Stories of EDUINFLUENCE

10 Life-Changing Powers to Unleash in Your School

Brent Coley

Stories of EduInfluence:
10 Life-Changing Powers to Unleash in Your School
Brent Coley

Published by EduMatch®
PO Box 150324, Alexandria, VA 22315
www.edumatch.org

© 2019 Brent Coley
All rights reserved. No portion of this book may be reproduced in any form without permission from the publisher, except as permitted by U.S. copyright law. For permissions contact sarah@edumatch.org.

These books are available at special discounts when purchased in quantities of 10 or more for use as premiums, promotions fundraising, and educational use. For inquiries and details, contact the publisher: sarah@edumatch.org.

Factoria W00 Demi font made from oNline Web Fonts is licensed by CC BY 3.0

Dedication

To my beautiful wife, my first editor and constant encourager. I could not have accomplished the task of writing this book without you by my side. Thank you for believing in me and for reminding me my stories are worth sharing. Most of all, thank you for loving me. I am better because of you.

To my children, Meghan and Ben. This book is about the influence we have on those around us. Know that you inspire me to be a better father and person each and every day. Your caring hearts and love for each other and others serve as an example and encouragement to me to be better for you. I could not be more proud to be your dad.

To my parents, my first teachers. Thank you for modeling what it means to be a person of character, for instilling in me the value of hard work, and for putting Christ first in your lives. You are my examples. You are my heroes.

Table of Contents

FOREWORD	1
INTRODUCTION	5
THE POWER OF A NAME	11
THE POWER OF RELATIONSHIPS	23
THE POWER OF EXAMPLE	35
THE POWER OF SHARING	45
THE POWER OF BELIEF	57
THE POWER OF APOLOGY	67
THE POWER OF APPRECIATION	77
THE POWER OF THE LITTLE THINGS	91
THE POWER OF FUN	107
THE POWER OF CONVICTION	119
THE POWER OF THE EXTRA MILE	135
UNLEASH YOUR EDUINFLUENCE	149
THE POWERS OF EDUINFLUENCE	155
ACKNOWLEDGMENTS	157
ABOUT THE AUTHOR	163

Foreword

    I have known Brent for many years, and as I read this book, I could hear his voice shine brightly through the pages. While you grow to know him more through each chapter, you will recognize that he contributes to the educational conversation with both honesty and integrity. Brent is vulnerable and willing to share even his most enthusiastic failures with his readers, because he knows it is how we respond to failure that shapes us.

    Throughout his book, Brent shares stories that remind each of us, teacher, administrator and parent alike, that schools don't just produce outcomes — they help raise children. He reminds us that teachers aren't technicians, trained to follow a manual; they are artists and influencers of our society's most important assets. For 20 years I have been lucky enough to serve as a part of the educational landscape of California, and during this time, I have watched the pendulum swing in the direction of accountability and "eduspeak" that can sometimes make schools feel more like corporate boardrooms than the caring second homes we wish upon our students and teachers.

    Stories of EduInfluence beautifully brings the education conversation back on course. With vulnerability that will make you blush, Brent shares stories from the edusphere that entertain, engage and

FOREWORD

unpack critical practices key to the success of anyone in the education field. While there are countless books that either focus on the skills needed to be a great educator or the stories that come from years of experience in the field, Brent weaves together both to ensure that every technique is wrapped up in an unforgettable story.

The term *EduInfluence* demonstrates the impact we have as educators: the power that our attitudes have on students, the importance of our relationships, and a reminder that the aftereffects of our interactions have long-lasting repercussions, shaping the lives of our students in ways that we may never know. EduInfluence is more than a return to the heart and art of teaching and leading in education. Brent creates with this book an intersection where the core values of education meet the craft of research-based strategy.

Some of the stories Brent unpacks are as recent as his reflections describing the influence of Twitter connections on his practices as a school principal. Other stories date back to his days as a classroom teacher when his learning space only had a single computer. Regardless of the era, each page of his narrative is just as relevant as it is informative, irrespective of the role in which you serve in education. If you are a teacher reading this book, you will relate to Brent's stories from his years of classroom teaching, like the time his admin walked in to observe him during a less than flattering instructional moment. For administrators, this book is chock-full of truthful recollections about leading a school that will resonate with any eduleader.

Unlike a cartload of teacher training manuals sitting on my shelf, this book is founded on the premise that we learn best through story and relationship. Stories help us learn and grow. They remind us that raising children, leading staff, and developing professionals is far more organic than mechanic. *Stories of EduInfluence* shines a spotlight on that elusive space between the freefall of working with children and the structures needed to be successful. While powerful techniques are introduced throughout, nothing is proposed without also being attached to an authentic experience that will both resonate with any educator and create a memory that can be drawn upon when developing your practice.

For me, one of the most memorable stories of the book was Brent's recollection of an encounter he had out in his community. Virtually every educator will relate to this "Oh, no!" moment that did not end well. However, Brent takes this nightmarish situation and wraps a lesson around it that is as useful as it is unforgettable. Throughout this entire book, Brent curates vulnerable moments like these that expose the realities of life as an educator, while grounding them in pedagogy-shaping lessons that I wish upon every educator.

Brent's willingness to let his readers peek behind the curtain and live vicariously through both his successes and setbacks is what makes this book such a treasure. His book will inspire you to continually grow

FOREWORD

your practice using the various facets of your EduInfluence. More importantly, you will have met a truly inspirational educator. When you put this book down, you will know his voice and you will feel as if you have made a friend whose advice you can rely upon.

- ***John Eick***
Executive Director of Westlake Charter School

Introduction

> *"If you've heard this story before, don't stop me, because I'd like to hear it again."*
> — *Groucho Marx*

Stories. Nearly everyone loves a good one. Stories engage us. They help us remember things. Stories can make us laugh and they can make us cry. They have the power to make us *feel*.

When I'm in church, I love when my pastor tells a story to illustrate a point in his message. Every time he utters a phrase like, "A few years ago" or "Let me tell you about the time when," my ears perk up. I lean forward in my chair. *Every* time. Why? Because I know a story is coming. I know he's about to drop some truth on me in a fashion that will not only be entertaining but long-lasting.

Storytelling is an extremely effective instructional strategy, but don't just take my word for it. Research has shown that listening to a good story can cause the brain to produce cortisol and oxytocin, neurochemicals responsible for increasing focus and creating feelings of connection and empathy (Zak, 2013). Focus. Connection. Empathy. Ingredients for making learning memorable.

INTRODUCTION

Did you ever have a teacher who was a master storyteller? I did. It was my first year of college in a history class. I don't remember the professor's name, but what I do remember is that during every single class — *every single class* — he had me on the edge of my seat as he masterfully spun tales of the Magna Carta and the fall of Constantinople. I don't remember him ever using notes. He just stood at the front of the room, periodically making illustrations on the chalkboard (yes, a chalkboard) and passionately took content many would consider boring and made it come alive.

So what's better than a good story? A story with a message. That's my goal for this book. I love sharing. I *really* love sharing. Writing that reminds me of Weston Kieschnick (@Wes_Kieschnick), one of my eduheroes, who says about himself, "I love teaching. No, really. It's a problem." That's me with sharing. I am a firm believer that the field of education is transformed when teachers, administrators, paraprofessionals — anyone who works with kids — shares their wisdom and expertise with others. This book is my humble attempt at making my contribution. I'm not sure how much wisdom I possess, but one thing I do know is this — after more than two decades in education, I have a ton of stories to tell.

A little background before we get started. I entered the field of education in 1996 and spent the first 15 years of my career teaching fourth and fifth grade in southern California. In 2011, I was given the opportunity to move into an administrative position in my district and spent the next two years serving as an assistant principal at the middle-school level. In 2013, I was again blessed with a new opportunity, this time to lead an elementary school as its principal. As I write this, I am in year six as the lead learner of Alta Murrieta Elementary (Go, Mustangs! #AltaRocks).

It's important to note that in the early part of my career, I had no aspirations to move into administration. None. Zero. In fact, when people would ask, "So, do you want to be a principal someday?" my response would be something like "Are you crazy? No way!" See, I became a teacher to be a teacher. I had no long-range plan that had me teaching for "x" number of years and then becoming a principal by a certain point in my career. I'm not knocking that mindset. Some people know that's what they want, set a goal and work hard to accomplish it. That just wasn't me. I wanted to be a classroom teacher, I became a classroom teacher, and a classroom teacher I would remain. Or so I thought. Administrators I worked under saw something in me I didn't see in myself and nudged me down the school leadership path. Though I initially resisted, I began to feel a calling in that direction. After several years, I answered the phone.

So back to the stories. Through my experiences in the classroom and front office, I have seen time and time again the incredible influence a teacher can have on the lives of children and the other adults around them. In a society fascinated with superheroes, I am reminded every day that the real superheroes live among us, wielding the superpower of **EduInfluence** in classrooms, front offices, cafeterias and on

INTRODUCTION

playgrounds. If you work with children, you are a superhero! Your words and actions have the power to shape the character of those you serve, to steer them toward greatness and to make them feel loved. This is an awesome responsibility and we have two choices when it comes to how we respond. We can 1) choose to be completely freaked out by this ("Oh, my goodness! What if I mess them up?") or 2) embrace the challenge and say to ourselves, "What an opportunity!"

This book is divided into chapters, each focusing on a unique power you possess, a facet of your influence. Each power is centered on a particular belief, a belief that if embraced, can transform your practice. To illustrate these powers, I'll share stories from my experiences, both successes and failures. We learn more from our mistakes than from hitting the bullseye and, believe me, I've missed the target more times than I'd like to admit. It's my hope that by sharing my stories, even the ones I'm not proud of, I can help others become better educators. Student names have been changed to preserve their anonymity, but every story you read actually happened. There's no fiction here. At the end of each chapter you'll find questions for reflection to help you take what you've read and apply it in your own classroom, office or at home with your own kids.

If you're looking for a book written by someone who has this education thing all figured out, I hope you saved the receipt. Sorry, but that's not me. I'm just a guy who loves kids, loves his job, has learned a few things over the years, and is looking to share what he's

STORIES OF EDUINFLUENCE

learned. But if you're an educator who has ever become discouraged and asked yourself, "Am I making a difference?" this book is for you. If you're looking for some encouragement and inspiration conveyed through stories that will make you smile, laugh and even cry, this book is for you. Because you *are* making a difference. You are powerful, more than you realize. You are a life changer, a superhero filled with EduInfluence.

So grab a cup of coffee or your favorite drink and settle into your favorite chair. It's story time!

Chapter 1
The Power of a Name

> *"What's in a name? That which we call a rose by any other name would smell as sweet."*
> — *Shakespeare, Romeo and Juliet*

What's in a name? A lot. While Juliet may argue that a name is unimportant, I have to disagree. A person's name holds immense value. It represents identity. For some, it's all they have.

If you have children, chances are when you were deciding on a name for your precious little one, you didn't choose it from the back of a cereal box. Your parents probably didn't do this either when deciding on your name. More than likely, it wasn't a decision made on a whim. In naming your own children, you may have wanted to use your own name, or a family member's, to honor someone you love. Perhaps you studied the etymology of names to find one that had a definition that really resonated with you. Names are important to people. Don't believe me? I just logged on to Amazon.com where a "baby names" search yielded more than 6,000 results in its "books" section. Over 6,000 books! Names are important and, in this chapter, I want to show you just how much power they possess.

Have you ever had one of those experiences when you encountered a student out in the community? You know, those times when a student sees you out of context, away from your campus, and has a look of utter shock on his or her face, because, in his or her mind, you're supposed to live at school? Several years ago, I had one of these experiences, and it beautifully illustrates the power a name holds.

What's Your Name Again?

One evening several years ago, I was out running some errands. After I'd finished picking up the items I needed, I hopped in my car and proceeded to head out of the parking lot, stopping at a red light at the exit of the lot. There I was, sitting in my car, with some music playing, just waiting for the light to turn green. As I sat there, I noticed movement out of my peripheral vision to my left.

In the back seat of the car next to me was one of my former students. She had the window three-quarters of the way down, and she was leaning her head out of the car. She excitedly called out, "Mr. Coley! Mr. Coley! Mr. Coley!"

Seeing a former student brought a smile to my face. You know the feeling. I turned the music off, rolled down my window and enthusiastically called out the window, "Hey, Christy! How ya doing?"

STORIES OF EDUINFLUENCE

The smile on the girl's face vanished, her excitement replaced by a crushed look.

"I'm Abby," she said in a forlorn voice.

Oh no! I said the wrong name! Terrible, I know, but wait — it gets worse!

Abby's car was in the left turn lane, while I was in the center lane waiting to go straight. Immediately after the words "I'm Abby" floated out of her backseat window, the left-turn light turned green. Abby's mom started to pull their car forward, leaving Abby clutching the window with both hands, a look of complete devastation on her face as she looked back at me and pulled away.

Clutching the steering wheel, I was left fumbling for words. "No! No! No! Noooo!" I cried as Abby's car pulled away, while I remained stuck at the red light, powerless to change the situation.

For you *Seinfeld* fans, you may remember the episode titled "The Pick." In it, Jerry was sitting in his car at a red light, and, unbeknownst to him, his girlfriend pulled up alongside him in a taxi to his left. Jerry proceeded to scratch the right side of his nose, but to his girlfriend looking on from his left, it appeared he was *picking* his nose. Jerry then turned to the left to see his girlfriend, a look of horror on her face. The taxi cab quickly pulled forward, leaving Jerry to cry, "No! No!" If you haven't seen or don't remember this classic sitcom moment, look it up on YouTube.

At that moment sitting in my car, I was Jerry. Abby had driven away, and I was powerless to communicate to her the truth. See, the truth was that I actually knew it was Abby. The crazy thing is, not only did I know it was Abby, I remembered her last name as well as both her parents' names. Christy was Abby's best friend. They played soccer together and, for whatever reason, when I saw Abby, "Christy" is what came out of my mouth.

Abby's name was important to her, and unfortunately, I got it wrong. I haven't seen Abby since that night. I hope she realizes it was an honest mistake and that I really did know who she was.

"I'm Special"

Fast forward a few years. I had the opportunity to move into administration and was in my first year as an assistant principal at a middle school. Like many administrators, one of my duties was to operate the front gate each morning as students came on campus. At 8:30 each day, I would open the gate and greet sixth-, seventh-, and eighth-graders as they arrived at school. While I was also checking for dress code violations, this was a great opportunity to build relationships with students, to let them know I wasn't just the guy who issued detentions to kids who got caught breaking the rules. It was a chance to look them in the eyes and welcome them — a chance to hopefully communicate I was an adult who cared about them. This was probably my favorite part of the day (well, not the dress code part).

Most mornings went something like this: Students would approach the gate, often in groups and I'd greet them with something like, "Good morning!" or "Happy Wednesday!" The majority of the time the most I'd get in return would be a grunted "Hey" or "Hi, Mr. Coley." Regardless of the responses (or lack thereof, as, after all, it's not always cool to talk to the assistant principal), I really enjoyed this time. But it wasn't until one winter day that I realized just how impactful this time could be.

One morning I stood at the gate greeting students just like any other day, when a few groups of students approached me.

"Good morning, ladies," I said to a group of three or four girls. "Good morning, gentlemen," to two boys right behind them. Then to a single boy a few feet behind the other young men, I said, "Good morning, Connor. Have a great day."

As Connor passed me, he mumbled something. Now, if you've ever worked with middle school students, a student mumbling something under his or her breath can raise suspicions. It wasn't like Connor to say anything inappropriate, but I confess I was a bit curious as to what he said.

Perplexed, I asked, "What was that, Connor?"

His response was not what I was expecting. He stopped, turned, looked me square in the eyes and said, "I'm special."

Now I was really confused. Connor was a great kid, but I was surprised to hear him say this, wondering what prompted his comment. He must have seen the confusion on my face, so he threw me a lifeline. "I'm special," he said again. "You said, 'Good morning, ladies. Good morning, gentlemen. Good morning, *Connor*.' I'm special," and he pointed at his own chest.

Boom! There it was. Wisdom from a 14-year-old. I called him by name, and in his eyes, that made him special. I was completely blown away. The simple act of addressing Connor by his name was enough for him to not just think, but audibly announce he was special. Looking back on my own teenage years, one of my greatest desires was to feel liked by others, to feel special. For Connor, it took one word to accomplish this — his name.

There is power in speaking a person's name. Do you like to hear your name said aloud? Unless you're in trouble with your spouse or your parent or are being summoned to the principal's office, my bet is you enjoy hearing your name. I do. When my wife says to me, "I love you," it feels good. I love it. But when she adds my name and says, "I love you, *Brent*," it takes it to another level. It's more personal, more intimate. Somehow it means something more. Can you relate?

I enjoy attending edcamps and educational technology conferences, and I go as often as I can. It's a great way for me to be inspired by, learn from and share with other educators who share my passion for kids and technology. I love it when I'm at a conference and run into someone I interact with on Twitter but rarely see face to face. What makes it even better is when the person greets me by my name. Every time this happens, it fills my tank. Like Connor, hearing my name makes me feel special. It makes me think to myself, "He knows who I am!" Have you experienced this?

My wife, Jill, and I recently discussed the power of hearing your name, and just the other day she walked in the house after picking up Chick-fil-A for the family and announced, "You're right! I love hearing my name!" She proceeded to tell me about how, since it was a busy time for the restaurant, a Chick-fil-A employee was out in the drive-thru taking orders and processing payments. Jill told me that after placing her order and paying with her debit card, she proceeded to drive up to the pick-up window where she was greeted by a different employee. Jill said she was surprised when the girl at the window cheerfully said, "Hi, Jill!"

Smiling, I asked my wife, "How did it make you feel?"

"Awesome!" she replied. "It's just my name. It's so simple, but it made me feel special."

As the principal of our school, one of my daily responsibilities and privileges is to supervise the drop-off loop at the front of the school as kids arrive. What a great way to start my mornings! I get to open car doors and, as I did at the middle school, greet smiling students with a "Good morning" or "Happy Monday" and wish parents a great day as they drive off. I get to high-five students as they walk up the sidewalk to the front gate. And whenever I can, I try to call students by name. Why? Because I want them to feel special. I want them to think to themselves, "He knows who I am." Is it working? You bet it is. I'll never forget the time I greeted a first-grade student by name as she walked up

THE POWER OF A NAME

to school. As she and a friend walked by me hand-in-hand, I heard the friend whisper in an awe-filled voice, "He knows who you are!" Names are powerful.

Before moving on, I have a confession to make. I'm not good with names. I'm great with faces, but I have a really hard time remembering people's names. At times, it almost feels like a disability. I know how important it is to address people, particularly my students, by name, but after the Abby incident, I'm understandably a little gun-shy about making the same mistake again. So I work at it. I work *hard* at it. If a student asks me, "Do you know who I am?" and I don't remember his or her name, I've learned to respond by saying, "Will you remind me of your name? Because I want to learn it." After the student tells me, I then follow up with, "I sometimes have a hard time remembering people's names, so if I forget tomorrow, will you remind me again, because I *really* want to learn it?"

I think this approach serves two purposes. First, it models to students that we all have strengths and weaknesses, even principals, and that we have to work at improving those things we struggle with. Second, it shows the students I care about them. I hope that it communicates to them, *"I may not know your name now, but you're important enough to me that I want to learn it, even if it takes a few tries."* I don't use people's names nearly as often as I should, but I'm trying. I've learned I can't live in fear of getting it wrong. I can't be afraid to exercise my EduInfluence because of the possibility of messing up again. Could I say the wrong name again and create another "Abby" situation? It's possible. But what if I get it right? What if I refuse to let my fear control me, speak a student's name and create another "Connor" situation? What if a single word, a name spoken aloud, causes another student to feel special? It's worth the risk.

Now, I've spent almost an entire chapter talking about the importance of speaking people's names, but before I close, it's essential to note there's something even more powerful than using a person's name — saying that name correctly. Pronunciation matters. Have you ever had someone mispronounce your name? I have, quite frequently. While it's difficult to mess up my first name, I hear my last name mispronounced all the time. Coley is pronounced *Co* (as in co-worker) *lee*. Cō•lēy. Long "o," long "e." Yet, more often than not, people seeing my name for the first time pronounce it with an "ooh" sound (as if it was spelled Cooley). At least half of my professors in college said it incorrectly, and now, it's one of my detectors for determining if a phone call I receive is from a telemarketer — "Hello, Mr. Cooley?" Nope, no Cooley here.

When people mispronounce my name, I don't get upset, but it definitely doesn't have the same effect as when someone says it correctly. It doesn't make me feel special, because what it communicates to me is that the person doesn't know me. The power in speaking a person's name comes in the connection felt when that name is uttered and heard. But it must be spoken correctly for this connection to be made. A name said correctly creates that "He knows me!" feeling. A name mispronounced does the opposite. What I've also learned over the years is that you have to ask how a name is pronounced, because students won't always correct you if you get it wrong. Some will be too shy to say anything, thinking to themselves, "Oh, that's OK." But it's not. When you take attendance on the first day of school, if you're not sure how to pronounce a name on your roll sheet, ask. We *must* get it right. Students deserve that.

If you're great with names, I envy you. Use your gift to speak life into your students (and anyone else around you) by using their names. If you're like me and recalling names is a struggle, remember that you're not alone. I encourage you to join me in doing whatever it takes (i.e., studying yearbook pictures, using mnemonics, utilizing Flipgrid so students can record themselves saying their names) to learn the names of those around you and then use those names to make people feel special. What's in a name? When spoken aloud and pronounced correctly, the power to make someone's day.

STORIES OF EDUINFLUENCE

Belief to Embrace:

There is power in speaking a person's name.

Questions for Reflection:

- Can you recall an instance when someone made you feel special by calling you by name?
- Has someone ever shortened your name or given you a nickname without your permission, producing a negative feeling in you?
- Have you ever positively impacted a student or adult by speaking his or her name?
- Have you ever addressed someone by the wrong name?
- Challenge: For the next week, when you're out in the community at Starbucks or any other retail establishment, take note of employees' name tags and call them by name in your interactions with them. See what kind of reactions you receive.

Tweet your thoughts and stories!
#EduInfluence

Chapter 2
The Power of Relationships

> *"No significant learning can occur without a significant relationship."*
> — Dr. James Comer

Let's begin this chapter by taking a walk down memory lane. Do me a favor and think back to when you were in school and identify a teacher you feel cared about you. Who was that teacher who treated you like more than just a name on a roster, who made you feel special? It could be at any level, elementary through college. If necessary, go ahead and put the book down and think about it for a few minutes. I'll wait.

OK, have that person in mind? Does thinking about him or her put a smile on your face?

While there are multiple teachers throughout my schooling who I feel cared for me, I want to shine the light on Dr. Andrea Guillaume, one of the block leaders in my credential program at Cal State University, Fullerton. She was also the professor for an educational statistics class I took during my master's program. Not my favorite subject, but Dr. Guillaume did an amazing job of putting the content into layman's terms, such a

THE POWER OF RELATIONSHIPS

good job in fact that I had earned an "A" going into the final exam. When she announced a few weeks before the end of the semester that students already having an "A" did not have to take the final and would receive that grade for the course, I had two choices: opt out of the test or put in some extra work and take the final. Tough choice? Not for me. I took the final. Didn't even hesitate in making the decision. There was no way in the world I was going to take the easy way out because, in my eyes, not taking the final would have let my teacher down.

See, in addition to being an outstanding instructor, Dr. Guillaume cared for me and the rest of her students. She made an effort to get to know us. She asked about our families, our interests, our jobs. She built relationships with us. So for me, I *had* to take the final, even though that decision led to extra studying and the risk of potentially lowering my grade. Her opinion of me meant that much. The story does have a happy ending — I did well on the exam and got my "A." I was proud of myself, but more importantly, I hoped my efforts had made Dr. Guillaume proud.

It's important to note that this was a graduate-level course and I was nearly 30-years-old at the time. The relationships teachers build with students aren't just impactful to kids. And just to illustrate how much this story is about Dr. Guillaume and not me as a student, I had the same opportunity in one of my other classes that semester to skip the final because of the grade I had going into the exam. I skipped that test. No relationship built, no desire on my part to go the extra mile. Folks, there's a lesson there.

Rita Pierson famously stated in her TED Talk "Every Kid Needs a Champion" that kids don't learn from people they don't like. Dr. Guillaume went out of her way to build a relationship with me, creating in me a desire to go out of my way to work hard for her. It doesn't matter how well we know the curriculum if we don't know our students. It doesn't matter how strong our pedagogy is if our classrooms and schools aren't built on the strong foundation of relationships. Unfortunately, I learned this the hard way during my first year of teaching.

"I Gotta Go"

If you're a classroom teacher, you know the importance of good classroom management. You understand it is essential for maximizing instructional time. If you happen to be a site administrator, you know that upon walking into a classroom, it takes about five seconds to determine the level of student engagement in that room. If learning isn't occurring, you'll know it and quickly. The greatest lesson ever devised will fall flat if students are off task and not engaged. Bottom line — if kids aren't listening, it doesn't matter what you're saying.

As a prospective teacher entering my credential program, I believed this. I still believe this. Classroom management is important. During my student teaching, I worked hard to develop strong classroom-management skills. I knew that if chaos reigned in my room, maximum learning would not occur. When I was hired for my first position to teach fourth grade, I established structure and routine from day one. We had fun in my class, but there was order. No swinging from the chandeliers in my classroom. I ran a tight ship, and I felt good about how things were going. That is until one of my students gave me a reality check, letting me know my priorities were misaligned.

One morning, all of my students were independently working at their desks, all except Arianna, who was at the back of the room working on the classroom computer. Computer. Singular noun. This was 1996, so there wasn't a row of computers along one of the walls of the room, and there certainly weren't any mobile devices. There wasn't even Internet in my classroom. Heck, the classroom had chalkboards, and for heat, we warmed ourselves by the wood-burning stove in the corner of the room. Just kidding. No stove, but the chalkboard part is true.

I was working on something near the front of the room when I looked up and saw Arianna standing before me. She quietly motioned for me to follow her to the front corner of the room as she appeared to want to tell me something privately. I walked with her away from the rest of the class, put my hands on my knees, and leaned forward to hear what she had to tell me. Arianna looked over at the other students to make sure no one was listening and then whispered in my ear, "Mr. Coley, I wet my pants."

"Oh, no," I whispered back. "Arianna, why didn't you ask me if you could go to the restroom?"

Her response, not at all what I expected, may as well have been a punch in the gut.

"I thought you'd say, 'no,'" she whispered, barely audibly.

Ugh. At that moment, I could not have felt any lower. I quietly sent Arianna up to the office to get a clean change of clothes and am happy to say that none of the other students ever knew what had happened. But I did. I was left to wallow in what I had done. *Congratulations, Brent*, I thought. *Look what your amazing classroom management has gotten you. Look what your precious structure and order have created — an environment where a student was afraid to ask you for permission to use the restroom because she thought you'd say, "no."* A 9-year-old, not a preschooler, wet herself because she wasn't comfortable enough to ask her teacher to use the bathroom. I cringe in shame as I type this, for as a first-year teacher, I didn't get it. I didn't see the full picture, but Arianna's words — "I thought you'd say, 'no,'" — opened my eyes. I realized at that moment that relationships are more important than good classroom management. If my students don't feel safe, if they don't feel comfortable, nothing else matters. As my friend Cori Orlando (@CoriOrlando1) has written, when we know better, we do better. I vowed right then to do better. I vowed to put students above structure.

THE POWER OF RELATIONSHIPS

Tears and Hugs

After the Arianna incident, I still didn't think classroom management should be thrown out the window. What I learned from my experience was that managing students shouldn't be my goal — *loving* them should be. Yes, it's important to establish a learning environment that is organized. Students shouldn't be left to their own devices, free to do whatever they want with no consequences. That's not good for anyone. But a management system cannot overshadow the relationships we build with our students (or adults if you're in a leadership position). They have to know, every minute of every day, that they are more important than a set of classroom rules. For those of you who, like me, value organization, structure and discipline, stay with me. It's not a "one or the other" type of thing. I've learned it's possible to teach students responsibility, to hold them accountable to a set of standards while at the same time letting them know you care about them. It's possible for students to feel loved in the midst of being corrected. Mark and Sara taught me this.

Mark and Sara were students in one of my fifth-grade classes who, though they were great kids with huge hearts, required a lot of attention. Both had amazing personalities that consistently made me smile, yet both also needed reminders to stay on task, to not blurt out, to stay focused. A *lot* of reminders. It's safe to say Mark and Sara received more support from me that year than any of my other students. Why? Because that's what they needed. When Mark was playing with something in his desk instead of working on his assigned task, I reminded him of what he was supposed to be doing. When Sara was doodling on a Post-It instead of reading her Literature Circle book, I gently guided her back to the text. To say this wasn't frustrating would be untrue. Honestly, the behavior of these two often tested my patience. They often made me laugh, and they often made me want to cry in frustration. You've been there. You know the feeling.

Fast forward to the last day of school. At the end of the day, after the final bell had rung, I dismissed the class for the last time, high-fiving students and wishing them a great summer as they left. After a few minutes of straightening up, I exited my room and headed to the office. As I walked, I noticed two students standing in front of another classroom nearby — Mark and Sara. All the other students had cleared out, so they were all alone. I approached and again wished them a great summer, but before I had a chance to walk away, Sara surprised me. She looked up at me and with tears in her eyes earnestly said, "I'm really going to miss you, Mr. Coley." She then threw her arms around my waist in a big embrace. As if Sara's actions were permission for him to proceed, Mark started crying, jumped forward and hugged me as well. "I'm going to miss you too," he said in a muffled voice, his head buried in my side.

So there I was, standing in the nearly empty quad, two crying students wrapped around my waist, telling me they were going to miss me — the last two students on Earth I would have expected to hear this from. If there were two students in my class whom I could have envisioned putting my picture in the bullseye of a dartboard at home, it would have been these two. If there were two students whom I would have thought couldn't *wait* to get out of my class, it would have been Mark and Sara. See, I had to redirect these two all year long. I had to be on them *constantly*. With as much attention as I had to give them, often in the form of redirection, I thought there was a decent chance they didn't like me, that they thought maybe I didn't like them. But this experience clearly showed me otherwise. Tears and hugs were not evidence of students who disliked their teacher. They were an indication that I had made a connection with them, despite having frequent negative interactions. They were proof that Mark and Sara knew I cared about them. I had made a difference. So many years before, my experience with Arianna taught me to put relationships over rules. Over a decade earlier, I had vowed to do better. At least with Mark and Sara, I had. I've received a lot of hugs in my career, but few more special than those from these two students.

R-E-S-P-E-C-T

One final story to illustrate the incredible impact of building relationships with students. When I was a middle school assistant principal, I frequently interacted with an eighth-grade student who struggled with showing respect toward adults. His name was Kevin, and he was frequently referred to me for being defiant. One day, Kevin was sent to the office for talking back to Larry, one of the campus supervisors, a staff member with whom he'd had several interactions of the less-than-positive variety.

When Kevin arrived at the office, I asked him to take a walk with me so we could escape the surroundings that are so often negatively perceived by students. I thought a neutral environment might help our conversation go a bit more smoothly. As we went to leave, I remember thinking something along the lines of, *"Dude, why? Why do you keep talking back to Larry? You know you're going to get in trouble. Why?"* But as frustrating as this behavior was, I had learned through my previous encounters with Kevin that getting openly upset with him, raising my voice, was not going to get me anywhere. Yelling wouldn't help the situation. As difficult as it sometimes was, when I spoke with Kevin, I always tried to keep my voice steady and calm. That's not to say I didn't express disapproval or that there were never consequences, that defiant or disrespectful behavior toward adults was tolerated. It wasn't. But I didn't yell.

On this occasion, after Kevin had honestly explained to me what he had done, owning up to his behavior, I voiced my earlier thought. I asked Kevin, "Why do you feel like you have to talk back to Larry?" His response has stuck with me ever since.

"Mr. Coley, you show me respect, so I respect you. Mrs. Kea (our principal) shows me respect, so I respect her. Larry doesn't show me respect, so I don't respect him."

THE POWER OF RELATIONSHIPS

Boom! For Kevin, it was all about respect. He didn't feel Larry respected him and in continuing my conversation with Kevin, he said he didn't feel Larry cared about him. There it is again. Another example of the power of relationships, or in this case, the lack thereof. No relationship built by the adult, no desire in the student to go the extra mile. This is another powerful reminder that relationships can be built and fostered even amidst negative circumstances. For Kevin, even when I had to correct and issue discipline, he still felt I cared about him, and his behavior toward me reflected that.

There is nothing in this world more powerful than love. The love a husband has for his wife. The love parents have for their children. The love teachers have for their students and the love those students give back. When you take the time to build relationships with your students, you lay the foundation for learning. To reach students' heads, we must first capture their hearts. Our students *must* know we care about them. This is not an option. Simply showing up for work and assuming they know is not enough. We have to be intentional. At the beginning of the school year, use an index card or Google Form to find out students' likes, interests, and one thing they wish their teacher knew about them. Then use that information throughout the year — don't just file it away and forget about it. One of your students likes to draw? Ask to see some of her artwork and spend some time really providing feedback. Have a student who plays soccer? Ask how her last game went. Better yet, go to one of her games.

STORIES OF EDUINFLUENCE

I spent a few hours one Saturday morning during my first year of teaching to watch one of my student's soccer games and his mother let me know years later that that simple act meant the world to him. If a student comes into class looking a bit down in the mouth, ask how he's doing. No, really. Not just a "Hey, you OK?" but a genuine effort to let him know you're there if he needs to talk. Remember, you may be the only adult in that child's life who gives him any attention. I don't want to be overdramatic, but in a society where teenage depression and suicide are all too real, your deliberate act of reaching out, your kindness, may save a life.

As educators, we are tasked to do so much more than simply teach students reading, writing and arithmetic. We have to constantly remind ourselves that we don't teach content, we teach kids. Those kids have to know we care about them. Students and adults will run through a brick wall for someone they love and who they know loves them. Love those you serve through your actions. Be intentional, and you'll leave a trail of crumbled brick walls in your wake.

THE POWER OF RELATIONSHIPS

Belief to Embrace:

Relationships are more important than rules.

Questions for Reflection:

- Who was a teacher who you knew cared for you, who made you feel special?
- Does he or she know? If not and you're still able, let him or her know.
- Have you had an experience like the one with Mark and Sara, where you discovered you made an unexpected difference with a student?
- What could you do to more strongly build relationships with the students or adults you serve? What steps could you take to be more intentional?

Tweet your thoughts and stories!
#EduInfluence

Chapter 3
The Power of Example

> *"A good example is far better than a good precept."*
> — Dwight L. Moody

"Do as I say, not as I do." Ever heard someone use that expression? Definitely not words to live by, especially if you're a parent, teacher or administrator. Really, they're not words to live by if you're anyone who is tasked to teach or lead others. Heck, let's be real. Unless you're Tom Hanks in *Castaway*, alone on a desert island, they're not words to live by, period. Why not? Because actions speak more loudly than words.

If you're a parent, you know this. You know that from the moment you bring your little bundle of joy home from the hospital, he or she is watching your every move. Those bright eyes, full of life, are taking in everything around them. They notice your smile, how you swaddle and hug them after baths and how you speak to your spouse. They're learning from day one, long before they're able to speak. Ever had your child copy something you do or say or imitate one of your mannerisms? Why is that? Because you're setting an example, even when you don't realize it. My parents set an outstanding example for my brother and me as we were growing up. Now in my mid-40's, I will at times say something in a way that prompts my wife to say, "You just sounded exactly like your dad." This makes me smile. Dad, if you're reading this, please know that's one of the highest compliments I can receive, to be told I act like you. Thank you to you and Mom for setting such a great example for me.

As educators, we need to remember that our students also watch everything we do — *everything* we do. Though I've had many experiences in my career reminding me of this fact, in this chapter I want to share two stories that really illustrate the power of our example, one from my time in the classroom and one from my experience as an administrator. Let's start with the most recent.

The Talent Show

Like many schools, ours holds an annual talent show toward the end of the school year. It's one of the highlights of the year for students, as those wanting to show off their skills get the opportunity to take the stage in front of their peers. Auditions are held, acts are whittled down, and the event is held on a Friday a week before school ends. It is so fun to watch students play piano solos, perform comedy routines, do dance numbers and sing their favorite songs. We have some amazingly talented kids at our school!

STORIES OF EDUINFLUENCE

A couple of years ago, the last scheduled act, the grand finale of the show, was to be a group of students dancing to the song "Watch Me (Whip/Nae Nae)." About a week before the show, the students in the act approached me with a question.

"Mr. Coley, will you dance with us during our act?" the leader of the group asked.

Before proceeding with this story, I must tell you that while I have many skills, dancing is not one of them. Seriously, it's painful to watch. If you're a fan of *Seinfeld*, remember the episode when Elaine dances? Remember how awful she is? That's me. I'm the male equivalent of Elaine Benes. The idea of getting up on stage in front of the entire school and showing off my "moves" (I shudder just thinking about that) was not very appealing to me.

"Will you dance with us?" they pleaded. "Please! Please! Please!"

How could I refuse those faces? I couldn't, so I agreed. A few moments of public humiliation would be worth it if it made my students happy. But now I had my work cut out for me, as while I had heard the song, I had no idea what the dance looked like. YouTube to the rescue! I remember watching the video over and over, trying to memorize the moves so I wouldn't look like a complete clown, even though I pretty much knew that was inevitable.

The big day arrived. The show was held outdoors with students sitting in the campus quad area and performers up on an outdoor stage where we typically hold weekly Friday Flag assemblies. As the finale grew

THE POWER OF EXAMPLE

closer, I made my way backstage dressed in jeans, a school t-shirt, and baseball hat to shield my bald head from the sun. The plan was that the students would start their act, dancing through the first verse, and I would then walk out from the shadows and join them, surprising the audience. The students took the stage, the song started blasting through the speakers, and they began dancing. The butterflies in my stomach grew into bats. I'm up on stage all the time in front of students, but this was different. Normally I'm passing out awards and making announcements. Now I'd be dancing. *Dancing* for crying out loud!

It was time. I stepped out onto the stage to surprised cheers from students and their parents in attendance. Looking over at the student dancers with a look of *"Nice job, guys! I think I'll join you,"* I reached up and turned my baseball cap around, because that's what you have to do to dance well, right? I was getting into character. The notes led up to the beginning of the second verse, and I started to bust a move. The students' cheers turned into screams of laughter. Parents grabbed their cell phones and immediately began immortalizing the moment for YouTube. But I kept dancing. It wasn't pretty, but it was fun. It was a moment the kids would remember, and that was worth a little embarrassment.

Of course, students flocked to me after the show, eager to comment on the spectacle they had just witnessed. I was bombarded by comments like "Nice dancing!" and "That was so funny, Mr. Coley!" Not surprising. But you know what I heard more than anything else?

"Mr. Coley, you broke the dress code."

Wait. What? I broke the dress code? I had just finished a dance routine without pulling a muscle (a fact I was very proud of), and they were talking about the dress code? I was confused.

"Mr. Coley," several students said, "You turned your hat around backward. You broke the dress code!"

You know what? They were right. Wearing hats backward is not allowed under our school's dress code. Busted! In my mind, I was getting into character, getting into "dance mode." But my students noted that my action contradicted what I had been telling them all year — hats must be worn facing forward. I didn't practice what I had been preaching. The example I set was poor, even though I didn't even realize I was setting it. It was a powerful reminder that students watch everything we do.

The Water Bottle

Another poignant reminder of the power of our example occurred way back in 2000. I was teaching fifth grade, and our K-6 school organized an event we called Literature Appreciation Day. In conjunction with Dr. Seuss's birthday, it was a day designed to celebrate reading. We set up a schedule so that in the morning teachers rotated to other classrooms in other grade levels to read aloud to students and later in the day, teachers performed Reader's Theater

THE POWER OF EXAMPLE

presentations for pupils. Students and staff came to school dressed in their pajamas, students brought pillows and blankets, and we pushed aside desks and chairs to create comfortable spaces for students to sit or lie while guest readers visited the classroom.

As a fifth-grade teacher, I was scheduled to read to a fourth-grade class, a different fifth-grade class, and a sixth-grade class. I was particularly excited to read to the sixth-graders because it meant I would have the opportunity to see some of my former students. After reading to my first two classrooms of students in fourth and fifth grades, I grabbed a bottle of water and headed to the sixth-grade class. When I arrived, all the pajama-clad students were sprawled out on the floor, lying on their blankets and pillows. At the front of the room was a stool and the book I was supposed to read. I walked to the front of the room and situated myself on the stool, the book in one hand and my water bottle in the other.

After about five minutes of reading, I stopped for a quick swig of water. I was holding the book in my left hand and the bottle of water in my right. Without setting the book down, I unscrewed the cap of the water bottle with the fingers of my right hand while still holding the bottle in the palm of my hand. Holding the unscrewed cap in my fingers, I proceeded to take a drink and then screw the cap back on — all with my right hand.

I began to read again but only spoke a few words before a student in the front row, a girl named Bailey, tilted her head back and said, "Oh! I *totally* remember that!" Bailey was one of my former students, and her comment came so soon after I began to read again that I knew she wasn't referring to the book. Confused, I asked her what she meant.

"You would always do that when you read to us," Bailey responded with a smile. She must have noticed the still-perplexed look on my face, so she continued. "When you would read to us, you always held a water bottle in your right hand, and when you would take a drink, you would always unscrew the cap with one hand, take a drink, and screw the cap back on with the same hand."

I was blown away. Up until that moment, I hadn't even realized I always held a water bottle when I read aloud, and I certainly didn't realize I held the bottle and unscrewed the cap with the same hand. I had never even noticed. But Bailey had. It's important to note that Bailey was a former student of not just one, but two of my classes. She was in my class when I taught fourth grade, and the following year she remained with me when I was moved up to teach fifth. That means Bailey was under my instruction for 360 school days, receiving countless lessons in math, language arts, social studies, science, and art. But on that day, what she remembered was that I always held a water bottle

THE POWER OF EXAMPLE

with one hand while unscrewing the cap with the fingers of the same hand.

Our students watch everything we do — *everything*! Like it or not, our every move is being observed and filed into students' memory banks. Whether you're a classroom teacher, instructional aide, librarian, or site administrator, it doesn't matter. They're watching. We are all actors on a stage, and our audience — students, their parents, colleagues — are watching us perform. But we are also the playwrights. We get to write the script. We get to decide what kind of play the audience sees. If our students are watching everything we do, let's choose to be intentional about what they see and hear. Let's take advantage of the opportunity to model manners, virtue, and good character.

What are the students and adults you serve going to see and remember? What script are you writing? Maybe they'll remember how you always hold the door open for your colleagues. Maybe they'll remember how you always speak kindly to that one student whom all the other teachers don't have any patience for (yeah, kids notice stuff like that). Maybe what they'll remember is the simple fact that you make the conscious choice to smile, no matter what kind of day you're having.

What will it be? The beautiful thing is we get to decide what our students and colleagues see. The fact is, those around us are going to remember what we do. As was the case with me turning my hat around at the talent show and with Bailey and the water bottle, it will

STORIES OF EDUINFLUENCE

often be the little things we may not even realize we're doing. So what's it going to be? What's your "Water Bottle Moment"?

THE POWER OF EXAMPLE

Belief to Embrace:

Our students watch everything we do.
What an opportunity!

Questions for Reflection:

- Has a student or colleague ever pointed out something you do that you weren't aware of? What was it?
- What do you think your students and colleagues are noticing and remembering about you?
- What is one thing you'd like to start consciously doing, something you'd like to be remembered for?

Tweet your thoughts and stories!
#EduInfluence

Chapter 4
The Power of Sharing

*"The miracle is this:
the more we share, the more we have."*
— *Leonard Nimoy*

From the time we were old enough to have play dates with our toddler friends, our parents taught us to share (or at least I hope they did). If you're a parent, you know sharing isn't something that always comes naturally to children. Sit and watch a group of 3-year-olds playing with toys, and you're bound to hear the words *my* or *mine* more than once.

"Hey, that's *my* doll!"

"Give it! That's *mine*!"

I haven't conducted any research on the subject, but in my experience, as a parent and teacher, it seems many young children have an internal fear that if they give up what they have, they're not going to get it back. They don't have enough life experience to know otherwise. As parents and teachers, it's our job to address this fear, to show them that sharing and taking turns are a necessary part of life.

THE POWER OF SHARING

So what about adults? While we typically don't have to worry about a colleague shouting, "Hey, that's my pen! Give it back!" in the middle of a staff meeting, how much of a conscious effort are we making to share what we have with others? I'm not referring to something like sharing the salt and pepper at a restaurant, but rather our resources and wisdom.

Many of us have Professional Learning Communities (PLCs) in our schools where time is set aside each week for collaboration with colleagues, but this time is often spent on tasks like reviewing student assessment data or creating formative assessments. Important stuff for sure, but too often I think this time is viewed by many teachers as the school or district administration saying, "OK, it's Monday. For the next two hours, meet with your grade level or department colleagues and share. Ready? Go!" In no way am I knocking PLCs and this time devoted to collaboration.

On the contrary, I think it's crucial. We're blessed in my district to have this time carved out each week for teachers to meet, plan and review student progress. In a profession where one of the most common teacher complaints (and a valid one at that) is the lack of time, scheduled opportunities for collaboration can be an incredibly important component of a school's success. But in this chapter, I want to go deeper. I want to encourage you to go beyond the regularly scheduled sharing time in your school. I want you to see how this facet of your EduInfluence, the Power of Sharing, can have a game-changing impact on others, even if they live on the other side of the world.

STORIES OF EDUINFLUENCE

My Virtual Mentor

I love technology. Growing up, I wanted to be a computer programmer and spent much of my free time in elementary and junior high school using the BASIC computer programming language to create simple, text-based video games with a couple of my friends. Yeah, I was that kid. So in the late 90's when it came time to choose a topic for the final project of my master's degree program, it made sense that I chose something combining two of my passions: teaching and technology. For my project, I chose to create a classroom website to enhance parent communication and improve student writing. I taught myself how to use Microsoft FrontPage and created a simple site called the Coley Chronicle Online. It contained basic information about the class, an "About the Teacher" page, and some student writing and artwork. Over the next decade, the site became known as **mrcoley.com** and grew into a large collection of resources for my students, their parents, and teachers all over the world (if you're interested, the site is still accessible, though it's no longer updated).

While building my site, I was constantly going online in search of other classroom websites. I wondered what other teachers were doing and hoped to gain ideas that could make my site better. Unfortunately, in 1999 there weren't a whole lot of classroom websites out there. Google Sites and drag-and-drop website creation tools like Weebly and Wix didn't exist, so it was difficult finding a lot of quality

THE POWER OF SHARING

sites. Then one day my educational world changed. I discovered Tony Vincent (@tonyvincent), another fifth-grade teacher with his own classroom website. It was awesome, exactly what I had been looking for. I emailed him to let him know how much I admired his work and to ask permission to adapt some of his resources to use with my own students and on my classroom website. He graciously gave his consent, telling me to borrow away. Over the years, I have continued to follow and be inspired by Tony's work as he shares ideas and resources at **learninginhand.com**. So many of the things I incorporated in my classroom and on my website (The Daily Blog, iPod flashcards, and ColeyCast, my students' classroom podcast) were the direct result of Tony freely sharing his ideas and resources.

Without a doubt, I am a better educator today because of Tony Vincent. He has a passion for learning and an equally strong passion for helping other teachers. Heck, Tony is the reason I'm on Twitter, and for those of you leveraging this social media outlet for educational purposes, you know what a game changer that is. Tony doesn't hoard his ideas and resources. Instead, he chooses to let his educational light shine. Because of that, I am among the thousands of teachers across this country and all over the world he has positively influenced.

Friends, here's the kicker — I've never met Tony.

Let me repeat that. *I've never met Tony Vincent.* He lives in Iowa. I reside in southern California. As far as I know, we've never even been in the same state at the same time, much less the same room. Yet, he's been a driving influence in my career through sharing on his website, Twitter and Instagram. I call him my virtual mentor, for although we've never met, technology has enabled him to teach me from a couple thousand miles away. I hope that one day I'll have the opportunity to meet Tony face to face, shake his hand, say, "Thank you" and buy him lunch. It'll be the least I can do for all he's done for me.

Are you doing for others what Tony has done for me? Are you sharing what you have? If you're not yet convinced of the Power of Sharing, maybe this next story will help persuade you.

18 Students in Alabama

Have you ever received an email that just made your day? Perhaps it was a message of appreciation from a parent or your administrator. Maybe you even hit the jackpot with a message from a Nigerian prince letting you know he wanted to give you $10 million. Woo hoo! All kidding aside, positive emails can buoy our spirits for days if not weeks, and several years ago I opened my Inbox to find a message that has encouraged me ever since. The message was from a teacher in Alabama teaching a class predominantly comprised of English Language Learners.

Before sharing her email, here's a little background. In her message, she referenced a note-taking strategy I frequently had my fifth-grade students use to help them remember information from

THE POWER OF SHARING

social studies lessons. I called them flowchart notes and similar to how a screenwriter storyboards his or her ideas, the technique had students break a story down into scenes. For each scene, students would write a short sentence describing what happened and then draw a picture to help them remember what they'd written (with vocabulary words underlined). I then posted photographs of these flowcharts on my classroom website for students to access at home. Examples of individual scenes and a complete flowchart can be seen below, and if you'd like more information on this technique, visit brentcoley.com/flowchart-notes.html.

STORIES OF EDUINFLUENCE

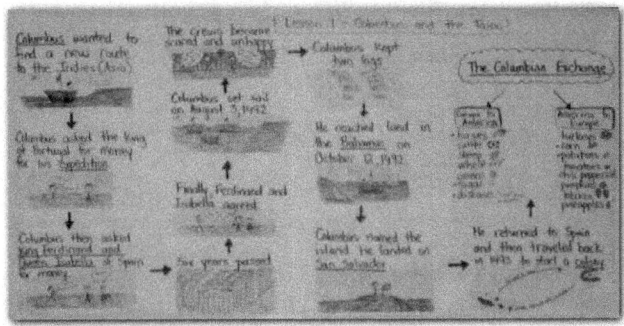

Here's an excerpt from the email I received:

> "I thought you should know that today you managed to touch the lives of 18 students here in Alabama. Last night I stumbled across your website and noticed your Social Studies flowchart on Columbus. Coincidentally, this just happens to be the lesson we are on. So, I thought I'd give it a try with my kids. Today is the first day my children ENJOYED Social Studies.

THE POWER OF SHARING

Today was the first day my students comprehended ANYTHING having to do with Social Studies. I just thought you'd like to know you made a difference in the lives of 18 children today, even though we are almost a continent away."

Wow! Talk about making a difference, and all I did was take a few pictures of what I was already doing in class and post them on my website. And my main goal wasn't even to share this idea with other teachers! I was simply looking to provide a resource for my students. But a teacher saw it and gave it a try with her students, apparently with very positive results. This opened my eyes to the Power of Sharing. These two stories beautifully illustrate that our EduInfluence extends far beyond our ability to impact just the students in our classroom or school. Our EduInfluence is global.

Time to deliver not one, but two truths.

what you have

Truth #1: Right now, someone is online looking for what you have. Let that sink in for a moment. There are more than seven billion people in the world, and right now, one of them is on his or her computer, tablet or phone searching for something you possess. Seriously, just think about that. Someone wants — no, *needs* — what you have. How many times have you gone online in search of the answer to a question or a YouTube video showing you how to do something? Other educators do the same thing. What separates teachers from so many other professions is that teachers are constantly on the lookout for something they can use in their classroom, something to better engage students and take their lessons to the next level. How many times have you found a teaching idea or resource on Pinterest, Twitter, Facebook, or via a Google search? My bet is more than once. So, are you contributing to that online treasure trove of educational goodness? Are you sharing?

Truth #2: You are somebody's Tony Vincent. You have the ability to do for someone else what Tony has done for me. *You* are somebody's Tony Vincent — or you could be. Through the miracle of technology, you have the power to share, to mentor, to encourage another educator, even if that person lives on the other side of the world. Now, I know what you may be thinking. *Not me. I don't have anything to share.* Not true! Do not believe that lie! You absolutely have something to share! This is not a time to be modest. You don't need to share something in a way that comes off as "This is the only way to do it" or "If you're not using _____, you're doing it wrong." Put it out there. If people need it, they'll take it. If not, they won't. But to deny others the wisdom, expertise or resource you possess because you don't think it's good

THE POWER OF SHARING

enough is not OK. What you have to share is too important. It could dramatically affect students you've never met, like the 18 youngsters in Alabama who tried flowchart notes for the first time. What you share could change the trajectory of an educator's life. That's not hyperbole. That's the truth.

Not sure what you could share? Need a few ideas? Here you go. It may be a note-taking technique like flowchart notes. It may be a graphic organizer you've found to be highly effective with your students. Perhaps it's a classroom-management technique or a book recommendation you think would be a perfect read-aloud or source of professional development. It may be the blog post you just wrote — or the one you've been thinking about writing, haven't yet, but should (consider this your nudge). It may be images of some student artwork that will inspire another teacher to try the project with his/her students. It may be a picture of your new classroom bulletin board. It may be nothing more than a few simple words of encouragement someone needs to hear/read. What you share may not have anything to do with education. I recently had the opportunity to speak about EduInfluence at a conference. After my keynote, a teacher approached me, introduced himself and proceeded to let me know he recently lost 80 pounds. He then told me that hearing the "Power of Sharing" part of my talk had inspired him to share how he did it. He let me know he had never considered sharing his story but now realized he must because someone out there could benefit from it. I was incredibly humbled, and it's my

STORIES OF EDUINFLUENCE

prayer this chapter will inspire you to contribute to others as well. If you're on Twitter, start there. Prefer Facebook, Instagram or Pinterest? Perfect. If social media isn't your thing, start in the teachers' lounge. It's full of people looking for ways to get better. Where and how you share doesn't matter. Choosing to contribute does.

You cannot say you have nothing to share, because that's simply not true. Are you letting others experience the genius inside of you? Are you sharing what you have? The world is waiting!

THE POWER OF SHARING

Belief to Embrace:

Right now, someone is searching for what you have. You are somebody's Tony Vincent.

Questions for Reflection:

- Who is your educational mentor, your Tony Vincent? If that person doesn't know about the impact he/she has had on you, let him/her know.
- What could you share with the educational community?
- What's holding you back from sharing?
- What is one way you could broaden your influence?

Tweet your thoughts and stories!
#EduInfluence

Chapter 5
The Power of Belief

> *"My teacher thought I was smarter than I was, so I was."*
> *— 6-Year-Old*

Have you ever gone to attempt something and just knew you would be successful? Maybe it was a free throw in a basketball game, and you had that can't-miss feeling, or perhaps you were standing over your golf ball, driver in hand, and just knew you were going to crush it right down the middle. That's a wonderful feeling. And if you had that feeling, my guess is you probably made the basket and hit a great drive.

Conversely, have you ever had the opposite feeling, where before you attempted something, a nagging doubt in the back of your mind whispered discouraging thoughts? *"You can't do this. You're going to fail."* That, on the other hand, is a miserable feeling. I remember battling those negative thoughts in a soccer game during my senior year of high school. The game had gone to a shootout, and my coach had chosen me to take one of the penalty kicks. I can still recall walking up toward the goal, and as I prepared to take the shot, I was bombarded by negative thoughts. *"You're going*

THE POWER OF BELIEF

to miss. You're not good enough to make this shot. That goal sure looks small, doesn't it, Brent?" I stepped up to the ball with all the confidence a member of the chess club has as he prepares to ask out the homecoming queen — not much. I stepped up, kicked the ball ... and it sailed over the goal. *Sailed* over the goal. You could have stacked another goal on top of the first, and the ball still wouldn't have come close to going in. I listened to my doubt, and it won the battle.

But during a two-man volleyball tournament in college, I had the opposite experience. My partner and I were playing quite well during the early rounds of the tournament, and this buoyed my confidence. As the tournament progressed, I became more and more confident, and by the time we played in the semifinal game, I felt like I could hit any shot I wanted. And I did. I remember my partner looking at me wide-eyed, amazed at the shots I was hitting, like he couldn't believe what he was seeing. Confidence flowed through my veins. I believed I could, so I did.

Belief is a powerful thing. It can propel us to accomplish things we didn't know we were capable of, but a lack of belief can paralyze and prevent us from reaching our potential, from becoming what we're destined to be. Several years ago I found out just how powerful belief can be, in of all places, a Walmart.

What Did I Do?

One summer day several years ago, I again encountered a former student and his parent out in public (don't worry, this time I got the names right). I was in my local Walmart picking up a few items, when walking down the aisle toward me, I saw a former student, Jack, and his mom. It had been a few years since I'd seen them both, so it was good to chat for a few minutes and catch up. Mom proudly told me Jack was in middle school now and doing well. I congratulated him on working hard and let him know I was proud of him, eliciting a quiet "Thanks, Mr. Coley" from the boy who was now nearly as tall as me. The conversation then shifted to Jack's older brother, Derek, whom I had also taught a few years before Jack. Mom proceeded to let me know that Derek was now in high school, playing football and getting great grades. Suddenly, tears welled up in her eyes and emotion nearly overtook her. "Thank you, Mr. Coley," she said through her tears. "Thank you for all you did for him. He would not be where he is today if it weren't for you." The next thing I knew, she had thrown her arms around me in a thankful embrace.

Well, that wasn't what I expected during my shopping outing, but there I was, standing in the main aisle of Walmart, hugging a crying mother as her son looked on. I thanked her for the words of encouragement and said it had been a pleasure teaching both her boys (it truly had been). Before going our separate ways, I wished Jack a great upcoming school year and asked his mom to tell Derek "Hello" for me and that I was proud of him, too.

There is a part of me that doesn't like to tell this story for fear it will come off as self-congratulatory

THE POWER OF BELIEF

("Look what a great teacher I am!") when that isn't the case at all. Quite the opposite. See, for the remainder of my time in the store, I thought back to the year Derek was in my class. I tried to replay all my interactions with him and, after doing so, a single question came to mind — "What did I do for Derek?" I thought and thought and thought and each time came back to the same answer — nothing. The mother of a former student had just expressed an incredible appreciation for all I had done for her son, but when I tried to think of what that was, I couldn't come up with anything.

See, when I asked myself that question, I was really thinking, "What was the *extra special* something I did for Derek?" Visions of Jaime Escalante in *Stand and Deliver* and John Keating in *Dead Poets Society* popped into my head. Upon comparing myself to those two teaching icons, I came up short. Way short. Sure, I had worked with Derek, a student who also received additional support. I hadn't left him to fend for himself. I remember sitting with him as he took some of his tests, reading the questions to him, as this was one of the accommodations in his IEP. I remember encouraging him when he became frustrated. I had provided him with the support he needed. But I didn't provide before-school tutoring for him every morning. I didn't give up all my recesses and lunches to work with him, and I didn't make home visits. I certainly didn't stand on my desk during class and recite poetry or hold extra classes on Saturdays, which is what all above-and-beyond teachers do, right? At that moment, that's what I thought amazing teachers did and I hadn't done any of those things for Derek.

When I had finished my shopping, walked to the parking lot and got in my car, it suddenly hit me like a bolt of lightning. New memories started rushing back that I hadn't previously recalled and I realized what I had done for Derek. It was so simple. I had believed in him.

I looked back at that school year and remembered how, a few weeks into the year, Derek came up to me with an assignment and asked me if he had to do all of it. A little surprised by his question, I responded by saying something like, "Yep. You can do it, buddy." Derek walked back to his desk and completed the task, albeit slowly. I didn't think much of the exchange until a few days later when he came up to me with a different assignment but the same question — "Do I have to do the whole thing?" Again, I was surprised by the question. Again I responded with something along the lines of, "Yes. If you need any help, Derek, let me know, but you got this, dude. You can do it." When he asked me the question a third time about a week later, I remember wondering, *"Why does he keep asking me if he has to do the whole thing?"* The answer came quickly — because he hadn't had to do entire assignments in the past. I asked Derek why he kept asking if he had to do everything on the page, and he told me that his previous teacher had frequently crossed off certain problems on assignments, telling Derek not to worry about them. Suddenly it all made sense. Derek had become accustomed to not having to

THE POWER OF BELIEF

do everything because his teacher had told him he didn't have to. Unfortunately, by doing this, I strongly believe his teacher was also unwittingly sending a message to Derek — you don't have to do all these problems because you *can't* do all these problems. Though unintended, I feel she communicated to Derek a lack of belief in what he was capable of.

Before I move on, I want to make it clear that I am not against modifying learning tasks or the conditions under which they are completed. Sometimes modifications and accommodations must be made to meet individual students' needs. That's what it's all about — meeting students where they are. That being said, I believe my experience with Derek illustrates that we must be careful concerning the unintentional messages we may be sending when we simply cross off problems or tell select students, "You don't have to worry about these."

So back to the original question — what did I do for Derek? I set high expectations for him. Did he need assistance, perhaps more than other students in the class? Sometimes, and when he did, I provided it. I worked with him, often one on one, but more than that I encouraged him. When he scored well on a test, I praised him, and when he struggled with a concept, I let him know he would get it with more practice. He saw I set the bar high for him, which meant I must have believed he could reach that bar. And he did. Derek did well that year. In a pre-standards-based grading era, he earned mostly B's, a few C's and even some A's. He worked hard, and it paid off. Though I didn't realize it at the time, I firmly believe that combined with his strong effort and positive attitude, a key component to Derek's success was the simple fact that in his eyes, I treated him like everyone else. I believed in him.

In the introduction of this book, I referenced how the principals I worked for early in my career saw something in me I didn't see in myself. They encouraged me to pursue my administrative credential to open doors down the road. They expressed their belief in me, but more than that, they acted on that belief and gave me opportunities to grow. They recommended me for committees, included me on leadership teams and made me the admin designee in their absence. They didn't just *say* they believed in me, they *showed* me they believed in me. Their encouragement and actionable trust were large factors in my decision to pursue more leadership opportunities. *If they think I can do it, maybe I can.*

About six years ago, I had a similar experience with expressed belief. I was completing my second year as a middle-school assistant principal and was asked to come down to the district office one morning toward the end of the school year to speak with the superintendent. While that could have been an "uh, oh" moment, I didn't think I was in trouble. I had heard that one of the elementary-school principals in the district was going to be moving up to fill an open middle-school principalship. In trying to figure out how the dominos would fall, it made sense to me that a current elementary assistant principal would be promoted to fill the vacant principal position, opening

THE POWER OF BELIEF

up an elementary assistant principal spot. Since I had expressed a desire to eventually move back to the elementary grades where I spent all of my teaching career, I wondered if perhaps this was why I was being summoned. I thought maybe district leadership was thinking of moving me down to fill what I thought would be an open assistant principal position at an elementary school. This was not the case. When I arrived, I learned that while the superintendent did have a plan for moving me, he wanted me to fill the open elementary *principalship*.

To say I was shocked would be an understatement. I'd only been an assistant principal for two years, and in my mind, there were several others with more experience and qualifications than me. I hadn't even dreamed of becoming a principal that quickly, but there I was, sitting in the superintendent's office, being told that's what he wanted to happen. I'm certain my open-mouthed expression gave away my surprise, and what my superintendent said to me is forever etched in my memory — "I know you don't think you're ready, Brent, but you are." He was right. I didn't think I was ready. Not even close. But he did, and he didn't just say he thought I was ready, he acted on it. I've now in my sixth year as the principal of Alta Murrieta Elementary. There are days when I still don't think I'm ready, but the faith and trust my district has placed in me, its belief that I can do this, helps carry me through.

I hope that sharing these stories will encourage you to express your belief in the students (or adults) you serve. This belief can and should be expressed not only through the spoken or written word, but also through our actions. Is it important to intentionally tell our students we believe in them? Absolutely! But if those words aren't accompanied by action, then the words are meaningless. Talk is cheap. "You can do it" and "I believe in you" should be phrases we utter early and often, but they'll ring hollow if students don't see us *act* like we believe in them.

So what might this look like? Maybe it takes the form of recommending a student for an advanced class next year because you can see the student's current performance doesn't match his or her potential. Perhaps you put a discipline-prone student in charge of something in your classroom, giving the student a responsibility another teacher has never bestowed upon him or her. Or maybe you encourage a student to check out that particular book he or she has an eye on, even though it may be a little above his or her reading level.

How much do you believe in your students? If you're a teacher, does every student in your class know you believe in them and do your actions demonstrate that belief? Do you hold high expectations for *every* student, believing that all students can achieve at high levels? If you're a site administrator, does every student in your school have an adult they feel believes in them? Not sure? Ask them. Belief is a powerful thing. It's difficult to accomplish much without it, but with it, the sky's the limit.

THE POWER OF BELIEF

Belief to Embrace:

Belief is the first step toward success or failure, in our students and in ourselves.

Questions for Reflection:

- How do you express belief in your students?
- Looking at your daily interactions with students, are there any unconscious actions on your part that express to them belief or a lack of belief?
- How could you more intentionally express belief in your students?

Tweet your thoughts and stories!
#EduInfluence

Chapter 6
The Power of Apology

*"An apology is a lovely perfume;
it can transform the clumsiest moment into a
gracious gift."*
— Margaret Lee Runbeck

"I'm sorry."

Saying those words can be difficult. Actually, now that I think about it, saying, "I'm sorry" is easy. Saying it and *meaning* it — that's what's hard. One of the things that really frustrates me is watching or hearing the news about an athlete or other celebrity who has said or done something highly offensive, only to follow it up with a half-hearted "apology," often released via a spokesperson or Twitter. You know what I'm talking about. A statement that begins with something like "I'm sorry if my words or actions offended anyone ... " and then goes on to make an excuse. It's painfully obvious the person isn't sorry, rather just sorry he or she got caught, and the all-important public image is now taking a hit.

THE POWER OF APOLOGY

In my current position as the principal of an elementary school, I often have to speak with students who have made poor behavioral choices. One of the things we talk about is taking responsibility for their actions. I like to tell students it's OK to make mistakes. We all do, even adults. But when we make a poor choice, we have to admit our error and accept responsibility for it.

One of the things I *don't* do is force students to apologize because too often I've seen children say they're sorry when they aren't. Take this example, which you may have seen played out a time or two. A child, we'll call him Billy, says or does something unkind toward his sibling, Carl. Mom or dad says to Billy, "Say you're sorry to Carl." Billy, under the threat of repercussions from his parent, looks at Carl and says, "Sorry," yet the look on his face and the tone of his voice clearly communicate a lack of sincerity. Ever seen and heard something like this? A forced apology isn't an apology at all. It has to come from the heart.

When I speak with students about their less-than-acceptable behavior, our conversations often finish with an exchange like this:

Me: "OK, so what do you think comes next?"
Student: "Say, 'I'm sorry?'"
Me: "Are you? Are you sorry?"
Student: "Yes."
Me: "Are you sure?"
Student: "Yes."
Me: "Well, if you're sorry, I think apologizing to (insert person's name) would be a great idea. I think

that would mean a lot to him/her. But if you're not, if you're not really sorry about what you did, if you're just sorry you got in trouble, then don't say you're sorry. Because then you wouldn't be telling the truth. You'd be telling (insert person's name) you're sorry when you aren't, and that isn't right. Do you understand this?"

One of the most powerful things you can do is apologize to someone you've wronged. Not an "I'm sorry if you were offended by what I said" apology, but a sincere, "I'd do anything to take back what I did/said" apology. It's no fun admitting we've blown it, but as educators, we're going to blow it. A lot. We're going to lose our patience. We're going to say things we regret. I certainly have, more times than I'd like to admit, but it was during my third year of teaching that I made the most regrettable mistake of my career.

My Biggest Regret

Before I jump into this story, a quick question. Have you ever had a student who required a lot of you? Of course you have. But I'm talking about that student who *really* required a lot of you, that student who daily tested the limits of your patience. Ever had one of those in your class? Perhaps the student struggled with focus and required constant redirection. Maybe he/she struggled with impulse control and was always blurting things out at inappropriate times. Ever had a student like this? Now a follow-up question — have you ever had one of these types of students who, at the same

THE POWER OF APOLOGY

time, you absolutely loved? A student who could drive you *crazy* but melt your heart at the same time? I have. His name was Daniel.

It was a Friday about two-thirds of the way through the school year, and I remember it like it was yesterday. I was teaching fourth grade. The students and I had just returned from lunch, and I was at the front of the classroom preparing for the next lesson of the day while my students silently read at their desks. When all was set, I turned to the class and said, "OK, boys and girls. Please go ahead and put away your books. We're going to do some writing."

In hindsight, I recognize I didn't use a hook for the forthcoming lesson, something to engage my students and get them excited about what was to come. Simply announcing to students that a writing lesson is next on the agenda does not typically elicit cheers. On the contrary, it often produces groans. On that day, at that time, that's exactly what I received. But not from everyone. Just Daniel. He scrunched up his face and whined, "Awwww!"

And that did it. It had been another difficult day full of frequent reminders to Daniel to stay on task and not blurt out. My patience was gone. That whined comment was the straw that broke the camel's back. It sucked out the last ounce of patience remaining in me. I'm not proud of it, but that's where I was. And my response to Daniel was the biggest regret of my career.

I was standing right in front of Daniel who was sitting in the front row. I looked him right in the eyes and in an equally whiny voice as his, said, "Awwww!"

STORIES OF EDUINFLUENCE

I mimicked him.

No, I mocked him. I took his single word, that sound expressing how he felt, and out of frustration threw it right back at him.

His shoulders slumped. He dipped his head forward and buried his chin into his upper chest. And in that instant, it hit me as hard as a slap across the face. I had destroyed this nine-year-old boy. I had crushed his spirit. With a single word, I had taken Daniel's heart of gold and trampled it. Tears cloud my vision as I write this and remember the look on his face.

You sometimes hear people talk about moments when their lives pass before their eyes. At that moment, my life didn't pass before my eyes — Daniel's did. In that instant, I imagined Daniel as an adult, looking back on his schooling and I realized that I had just become "that" teacher, the teacher he will remember for the rest of his life — and not for the right reason. If we look back on our school years, we all have that teacher, that teacher we remember, the one who made a permanent impression on us, for all the wrong reasons. That teacher who was harsh with his or her words. That teacher who didn't believe in you. That teacher who mocked you. I had just become that guy to Daniel, and it ripped my heart out.

I shook myself from my thoughts, took a few steps to my left as I prepared to begin the lesson and stopped. I pivoted and walked back to Daniel's desk, my head down, and looked up at the class.

"Boys and girls," I said slowly. "What I just did was not OK. What I just did was wrong." I then looked at

THE POWER OF APOLOGY

Daniel, who was looking up at me with hurt in his eyes. "Daniel," I said in a soft voice but loudly enough for all to hear, "will you forgive me?"

"Yes," he instantly said with a small smile. The pain didn't completely leave his eyes, but they brightened just a bit. There it was, his heart of gold. Thankfully, it was still beating.

"Thank you, Daniel," I said with an impish smile.

Pulling myself together, I managed to teach that darn writing lesson (which I'm sure wouldn't have won any awards) and finish out the day. I have no idea how I did it, because every time I looked in Daniel's direction, my mind replayed what I had done. My heart ached. After what seemed an eternity, the final bell mercifully rang, I dismissed my students and then proceeded to have one of the worst weekends of my life.

That Sunday afternoon I went over to my parents' house for dinner. I recall catching up with my dad before our meal and recounting to him what had happened two days prior. I spilled it all, from Daniel's action to my response to my apology.

"Dad," I remember saying to him in anguish, "I blew it! I'm *that* teacher to Daniel now."

As he has so often done throughout my life, my dad responded with truth and wisdom. I didn't expect him to say what he did, but his words changed me as an educator and person. After a few moments of reflection, he said, "Or, you may be the first adult who has ever apologized to him. He may remember you for that."

STORIES OF EDUINFLUENCE

I staggered for a moment under the implications of that statement. Could that be true? It was definitely possible. I obviously wasn't the first adult to have ever made a mistake with Daniel, but perhaps I was the first one to have ever admitted the error and then sought Daniel's forgiveness. We all know we're supposed to learn from our mistakes, but my father's words resonated with me. Not only should we learn from them, but when our mistakes affect others, hurt others, we must seek forgiveness. As teachers, administrators, instructional aides, cafeteria workers, we're going to mess up with students. We're going to say and do things we shouldn't. What my experience with Daniel and my subsequent conversation with my father taught me is this — **when you blow it with students, own it, because it may be the action *after* your mistake that makes the difference.**

Kids are smart. When an adult makes a mistake, kids know it, regardless of whether or not the grown-up chooses to believe it. I'm not just talking about high school students either. Five-year-olds (and kids even younger) are capable of realizing when their teacher, principal or parent messes up. How we respond is what matters. Refusing to acknowledge our culpability, thinking we can't appear weak in the eyes of the child, doesn't make us strong. We consistently teach our students to take ownership of their learning and behavioral choices. How can we expect students to do this if we're not willing to do it ourselves? We must model what we expect. When a student makes a poor choice, we teach them the importance of taking responsibility for that choice. Are we practicing what we preach?

When you're working with students and make a mistake, apologize. When you lose your patience and respond to a student in a tone of voice that doesn't hide your frustration, apologize. When you jump to a conclusion and realize later you didn't have all the facts and falsely accused a student of doing something he hadn't done, apologize. Seek his forgiveness. When your joke doesn't land as you intended and your words instead cause a student to become embarrassed, apologize. And what makes that apology even stronger is to do it publicly.

If a sarcastic comment hurts a student's feelings, apologizing is the right thing to do, but seeking that student's forgiveness in front of his or her peers is even more powerful. It shows students you're human (which, by the way, they already knew). It demonstrates your pride is not more important than their feelings. Imagine what that kind of modeling can do in the development of the young people you serve. Imagine what that will do for your students who will one day grow up to become teachers, husbands, wives, and parents. As educators, we must always remember that we're teaching more than just the A, B, C's and 1, 2, 3's. We are shaping the character of those we serve, and our daily actions teach more powerfully than any formal lesson.

My sincere prayer is that my dad was right. Did I become "that" teacher to Daniel? Yes. I was an adult in his life whose actions were hurtful. But I was also

STORIES OF EDUINFLUENCE

willing to own my mistake and seek his forgiveness. I hope that Daniel remembers me for both reasons.

THE POWER OF APOLOGY

Belief to Embrace:

We're going to make mistakes with our students. How we respond afterward is the key to minimizing the impact of those mistakes.

Questions for Reflection:

- When was a time you blew it with a student?
- Have you ever apologized to a student? If so, what was the student's reaction?
- Is there a student you have wronged and to whom you haven't yet apologized? If so, what's holding you back?

Tweet your thoughts and stories!
#EduInfluence

Chapter 7
The Power of Appreciation

*"Appreciation can make a day, even change a life.
Your willingness to put it into words is
all that is necessary."*
— Margaret Cousins

Regardless of position, everyone wants to feel appreciated. No, everyone *needs* to feel appreciated. When you come to work, you don't do it for the glory. You're not expecting a standing ovation after each lesson or a parade at the end of the day (at least I hope you're not, because you're bound to be disappointed). You do it for the kids. You do it for those you serve. That being said, I think you'd agree it's certainly nice when someone lets you know your efforts are appreciated. When you're at work and a parent, colleague or supervisor lets you know he or she notices and appreciates what you're doing, doesn't it put a smile on your face, a spring in your step? In my experience, I've found it's hard to get in trouble for giving too much encouragement or appreciation, but the consequences of not providing enough can be disastrous.

THE POWER OF APPRECIATION

So what does this mean for us as educators? If you're a teacher, how can you wield the Power of Appreciation to lift up your students? If you're an administrator, how can you better encourage those you serve? It's simple. When someone you work with does something you appreciate, let him or her know. The form it takes can vary, but communicating that appreciation is non-negotiable.

At some point, you've probably had a thought similar to this — *"Wow! She's awesome! I'm so glad she's on our team."* If you have, don't keep thoughts like that to yourself. Tell them. Write them. Text them. Heck, use a carrier pigeon if you have to. How you communicate your appreciation doesn't matter. Making the conscious decision to convey that gratitude does. My friends Cori Orlando, John Eick (@John_Eick), and I have a Voxer group called "Appreciation People," in which we periodically record short messages to each other with the explicit purpose of building each other up. When we have something positive happen in our schools, perhaps a "light bulb" moment with a student, we share it. When things are difficult, we share it so our friends can offer us encouragement to hang in there. We've built a virtual way to brighten each other's day. I encourage you to create your own "Appreciation People" group, either on Voxer or in your text-messaging app. Choose a few people, create a group chat and start letting them know how much you appreciate them. Again, it doesn't matter how you spread the love, as long as you spread it!

STORIES OF EDUINFLUENCE

OK, OK. You might be thinking I'm making too big a deal of this. *It's just a few kind words, Brent.* Wrong!
You got the job.
They accepted your offer. The house is yours!
I love you.
Will you marry me?
We're gonna have a baby.

Are these just words? Of course not! These words, in this order, are life-changing and we can use our words to change the lives of those around us. A kind word, expressed at just the right time, can change the direction of a person's day, week or even month. In this chapter, I'm going to share with you three experiences that I pray will inspire you to use this facet of your EduInfluence to lift up those you serve. Don't be deceived — this is more than just being "touchy-feely." This isn't about leaving love notes for your spouse, though if this chapter inspires you to be better about that too, great! This is about being truly intentional about using our words and actions to breathe life into others, specifically our students and colleagues. And it's so easy to do! Don't believe me? Read on!

A Power-Packed Post-It

I love sticky notes. During my time as a classroom teacher, my students and I used them all the time. I leveraged this adhesive tool to keep myself organized, sticking reminders and checklists all over my desk, notebooks, and teaching manuals. My students had their own pads of sticky notes for a variety of purposes:

THE POWER OF APPRECIATION

note-taking, making graphs in math, and even classroom currency paychecks. They were everywhere in my classroom, and you'll find them all over my office today. Sticky notes are awesome, but a few years ago I saw just how powerful a Post-It can be.

One afternoon after school, a teacher and I were in her classroom talking. As we were standing by her computer, I glanced down and happened to notice a sticky note stuck to the bottom of the teacher's monitor. On it were the words *"Thanks for everything you do!"* I did a double take because the handwriting on the note looked familiar. For good reason — it was mine.

I remembered writing the note, but to be honest, I couldn't recall exactly when. What I did know was that I hadn't written it recently, yet there it was, stuck to her monitor, offering her encouragement every time she sat down at her desk. At that moment, I was reminded of the long-lasting impact words of encouragement can have. Five words, written on a sticky note. That's it. Not a five-paragraph essay, not a formal letter of commendation. A sticky note. Yet it was meaningful enough that it didn't get tossed in the trash. It instead occupied valuable real estate on her desk.

Seeing that sticky note has been a clear reminder that I need to write notes like this more often. I often think how appreciative I am of those around me and try to be very deliberate in expressing my appreciation verbally. That's great, but putting those words of affirmation in writing takes it to another level. A note is tangible. A note can be saved and read again and again and again. And again, many years later.

Do you have anything like this, a note you still have years after you received it? I do. Years ago I took an empty file folder and labeled it "Feel Good File." Since that day, every time I've received a nice note from a student, parent, staff member or administrator, I've dropped it in this folder. Periodically, I pull the file out and glance at some of the notes inside, usually when things are incredibly stressful, and I'm in need of a little encouragement. Most of the notes I've saved aren't long. Many are tiny scraps of paper with only a few words on them. But they've meant enough to me that I've saved them for all these years, and they've lifted my spirits time and time again.

Since much of the correspondence we receive nowadays is in the form of email, I also have a digital version of my "Feel Good File" in which I save encouraging emails. If you don't have something like this yet, I encourage you to create your own email and hard-copy versions of a "Feel Good File." While you're at it, create a bookmarked online version that can be accessed from all your devices, anywhere, anytime. Start preserving those words of affirmation for the days when you'll really need them.

If you're a classroom teacher, make it a priority to write notes like this to your students. Choose one student each day and write a short note of encouragement on a sticky note and put it on his or her desk, notebook, cubby, etc. It doesn't have to be long. "Thanks for coming to class with a smile each day!" "I appreciate your positive attitude!" That's all it'll take to make that student's day and chances are that note won't find its way to the trash. If you're an administrator, take a moment to write notes like this to your staff. It'll make a difference, I promise. And who knows? You may find your note stuck to a computer monitor someday.

You've Got Mail

Whether you're in the classroom, front office, or district office, you know that April and May are long months. While they may have the same number of days as their counterparts, these two months just feel longer due to the incredibly large number of things vying for our attention during the home stretch of the school year. State testing. District assessments. Preparing report cards. Planning end-of-year grade-level activities. Oh, and that little thing called "spring fever." If you work in the upper elementary grades, you're nodding your head right now because you know exactly what I'm talking about. Spring fever, the annual phenomenon where upper elementary boys and girls suddenly become aware of each other, making the life of teachers, administrators and support staff even more challenging than usual.

During this time of year, it's easy to become discouraged. We still love what we do, but we're tired. It's in times like these that a message of appreciation can go a long way. It did for me a year ago. It was mid-May, and I had just gotten home after a long, stressful day at school. I was spent. Worse, I was feeling like I wasn't making a difference. Have you ever been there? You're working hard, really hard, but you don't feel like you're doing enough. Can you relate? That's where I was, until I picked up my iPad. In my email inbox was this message from the parent of two of my students:

> *"You've been on my mind today, and I just wanted to reach out and thank you for everything you do for our kids, our school, and our community! You make a huge impact, planting seeds which you may never get to see all the fruit from. But you can be sure of the harvest! You are truly appreciated, my friend!"*

My reaction? I lost it. I was already on the verge of tears from the stress of the job, and this message sent me over the edge, in a good way. I was doubting my impact, and like manna from Heaven, this email had arrived in my inbox. It probably took the parent only a minute or two to write, but its effect was long-lasting. He probably thought his message would simply brighten my day, but it did so much more than that. It helped sustain me. It filled me with enough encouragement to get me through the last few weeks of the school year. His message was that powerful.

Whom do you work with who could use a message like this? Is it a student, a colleague, your administrator? (Yep, admin needs encouragement, too.) If a specific person comes to mind, put this book down for a moment and go write that person a note, email or text of appreciation. Don't put it off. It's too important. Don't let there be a chance of something sidetracking you. Do it now.

If you're a site administrator reading this, this call to action is doubly important for you. Teachers leave the profession every year because they don't feel valued. Don't let this happen to one of your staff members. Let them know you appreciate all the hard work they put in. It's not just possible but highly probable that at least one of your teachers is in desperate need of an encouraging word right now. You have the power to provide it. Don't let the opportunity pass you by!

"I Didn't Get My Walkthrough Form"

As a site principal, one of the joys of my job is having the opportunity to get into classrooms and see students engaged in learning. I thoroughly enjoy popping into rooms, even if just for a few minutes, to see the amazing learning experiences our teachers create for their students. I love my classroom visits! They are one of the best parts of my day. Unfortunately, I also understand that an administrator's entrance into a classroom brings with it the possibility of increased nervousness or anxiety on the part of the teacher. While I'm not there to catch the teacher doing something wrong, I get it. Supervisor walks in. Heart starts beating more quickly, even if for only a few seconds. I understand. I've been there. It's natural to want to put your best foot forward when someone walks into your room.

When I moved into administration as an assistant principal, I began using Google Forms for my informal walkthroughs. I created a simple form that I would complete with my iPad or phone after each classroom visit. The data from this form (e.g., teacher name, subject observed, what I observed) was then sent to a spreadsheet that helped me keep track of how many times I had visited each teacher's classroom. I had found a simple, efficient way to keep myself organized. It was great, or so I thought.

I'll never forget the afternoon during a staff meeting when one of our teachers told me that my walking into the room with my iPad was the equivalent of walking in with a digital clipboard. They knew what the iPad was for — the walkthrough form — but they didn't know what I was tapping into the form, what I was writing after my visit. They weren't getting positive feedback (even though I was seeing great things) and it was freaking them out. Unintentionally, I was negatively wielding my EduInfluence, and I knew I needed to make a change. I wanted my informal walkthroughs to be a positive experience for teachers, an encouragement, not something they endured. The Google Form was a great tool, but I needed to find a way to use it to not only keep myself organized, but more importantly, leverage the Power of Appreciation.

Fortunately, I discovered Autocrat (thank you, Jason Seliskar (@JasonSeliskar)). This free add-on for

THE POWER OF APPRECIATION

Google Sheets takes the information submitted through a Google Form and automatically merges it into a template you create. Pretty sweet, huh? But wait, there's more! In addition to magically creating this document, Autocrat can then automatically email it to a person (or people) of your choosing. It's amazing! In this tool, I had uncovered the solution to my classroom walkthrough dilemma. Now, each time I visit a classroom and complete my walkthrough form (which I now do on my phone outside the room to avoid the perception of a digital clipboard), Autocrat sends the teacher an email with a document like the one below.

I have chosen to use this process to intentionally build my teachers up, to let them know what they're doing in the classroom is awesome and appreciated. Again, I'm not there to catch, I'm there to affirm. Yes, if something's going on in the classroom that is concerning or inappropriate, we're going to have a conversation, but that's not what this form is for. This is an instrument of appreciation. By the way, if you're interested in learning how to use Autocrat for yourself, you can view a short tutorial video I created at bit.ly/autocrattutorial.

So how have teachers responded? They love it!

Wait, what? Brent, you're saying your teachers like it when you come in to observe their classrooms? Yep, that's what I'm saying. Through the magic of Google Forms and Autocrat, I've been able to take the traditional perception of classroom walkthroughs and turn it on its head. Teachers know that when I visit the classroom, they're going to get an email notification a few minutes after I leave, letting them know some words of encouragement are waiting in their inboxes.

Need proof? Recently, during our fifth-grade teachers' lunch break, I walked through the staff lounge, and one of the teachers said to me, "Hey, Brent. Casey and I were just talking, and we didn't get our emails." I stopped, a confused look on my face, so she continued. "You did a walkthrough in our rooms, but we didn't get the email with the positive note," she said with a smile. She was right. I had gotten sidetracked immediately after leaving their rooms and had not yet completed the feedback form for each of them. The great part? They noticed. And not only did they notice, but the encouragement they were used to receiving through these feedback forms was also missed, so much so that the teacher essentially asked me to complete the form, asked me to make her feel appreciated. So I did!

Now, let me ask you a question. When is the last time someone let you know you are appreciated? I'm

THE POWER OF APPRECIATION

not talking about a colleague thanking you for holding the door open or for letting her borrow some construction paper, I'm talking about someone communicating to you sincere appreciation for what you do or who you are. As I've asked you to do before, take a moment and really think about it. I'll wait.

If an instance quickly popped into your head, that's fantastic! Hopefully, recalling those words of affirmation lifted your spirits and reminded you that you are valued. The purpose of this chapter is to remind you that you have the power to create that positive feeling in those around you.

If, on the other hand, you struggled to recall a time when someone has spoken these types of words to you, it probably didn't make you feel very good. It stinks to feel unappreciated or overlooked. If you've ever felt this way, you're not alone. Too many people go through their days without ever hearing any words of encouragement. That's a problem. The good news is we have the power to change that. We have the capacity to ensure that no one we work with feels this way. **Expressing appreciation does for those around us what helium does for balloons.** It lifts them up. It keeps them afloat. You've seen a tired balloon that's lost its helium, just holding on, barely floating above the floor. At some point, I'm sure you've felt like that balloon, in need of a lift. Be that boost for those you serve. Don't let them be that balloon.

STORIES OF EDUINFLUENCE

Belief to Embrace:

Expressing appreciation does for those around us what helium does for balloons — it lifts them up.

Questions for Reflection:

- Recall a time someone unexpectedly expressed gratitude or appreciation for what you do. What was the situation, and how did it make you feel?
- When is the last time you deliberately expressed gratitude or appreciation for someone else?
- How do you typically express gratitude or appreciation to others, and how do you most like to receive messages of gratitude/appreciation (e.g. verbally, handwritten notes, text/email)?
- Which of your students or staff members do you think could use a boost in the form of some expressed appreciation? How could you express it?

Tweet your thoughts and stories!
#EduInfluence

Chapter 8
The Power of the Little Things

> *"Sometimes the smallest things take up the most room in your heart."*
> — *Winnie the Pooh*

Think about the last time you met someone new. Perhaps you were at a dinner party and … wait, hold on. Do people still go to dinner parties? I know people meet friends for dinner, but when is the last time any of us went to a dinner *party*? I'm not sure I've *ever* gone to a dinner party. Anyway, you're meeting someone new, and the conversation shifts to what you do for a living. When telling someone you're a teacher, the person is likely to respond in one of two ways. The first is a chuckled reply along the lines of "Oh, wow. Must be nice to have three months off every summer." Ever had someone say something like this to you? If so, were you tempted to deliver a five-minute "you don't know what you're talking about" lecture? If you did, I wouldn't blame you.

Fortunately, nowadays when someone learns that you are a teacher, the more common response is educated and sympathetic.

THE POWER OF THE LITTLE THINGS

"Oh, my goodness! I could never do what you do!"
"You don't get paid enough."
"That has got to be such a hard job."

When I meet new people and tell them I'm in education, a response like this is what I typically hear. Most people understand that teaching is a difficult job. I recently saw a quote on Facebook that made me laugh. It read "Teaching is easy. It's like riding a bike, except the bike is on fire. You're on fire. Everything is on fire." Yep, some days definitely feel like that.

Being a teacher is hard. Being an administrator is hard. There are so many aspects to what we do, and it seems every year more and more things get added to our plates and challenges we never or rarely faced just a few years ago are now commonplace. It's so easy to get bogged down with all of the responsibilities involved in doing our job well. Familiarizing ourselves with updated standards. Learning new curriculum. Differentiating instruction. Keeping standards-based grades. Attending IEPs and SSTs. Handling discipline problems. Should I go on? I could, but I think you get the picture. We are responsible for a *ton*.

While all those things are important — really important — the purpose of this chapter is to remind you that a large part of your EduInfluence lies in actions that are often overlooked. It's the little things that often have the biggest impact on the lives of the students and adults we serve.

Wait. Brent, you're saying there are things just as important if not more important than knowing the standards and differentiating instruction? Yep, that's exactly what I'm saying.

In preparation for writing this chapter, I reached out to my Professional Learning Network (PLN) on social media and asked them this question:

> **WHEN YOU THINK OF YOUR FAVORITE TEACHER IN SCHOOL GROWING UP, WHAT DO YOU REMEMBER MOST?**

I received several responses, but you know what no one mentioned? Learning how to do long division. Nobody talked about how their teacher individualized instruction either. In fact, nearly every reply from my PLN had nothing to do with curriculum or instruction. What they remembered were the little things. Here are a few of their memories:

"Kindness."

THE POWER OF THE LITTLE THINGS

> *"She was always happy and loved all her students, even the naughty ones."*
> *"I don't remember her ever raising her voice."*
> *"She cared."*
> *"She came to my house for dinner."*
> *"She smiled at me."*

Wow! *She smiled at me.* More than 20 years later, a smile was the memory that stood out most. Not pedagogy. Not content knowledge. A smile.

Reading these responses from fellow educators made me wonder — what memories do *my* former students have of being in *my* class? Fortunately, I'm Facebook friends with a handful of my former fourth- and fifth-graders, now college graduates (as if I needed another reminder of my advancing age), so I decided to reach out and ask them what they remembered. I asked them to honestly share what memories stand out from being in my class. I told them I wasn't fishing for compliments. If all they remembered was that I always wore blue shirts, that's what I wanted to know. I predicted their memories would be much like those of my PLN, that they wouldn't include specific lessons but rather be about things considered to be non-academic. You know, the little things. Here's what they said:

> *"I remember you smiled a lot and kept the classroom atmosphere enjoyable/positive."*

STORIES OF EDUINFLUENCE

"You had excellent penmanship when you wrote on the whiteboard."

"I remember coming into your classroom after lunch, and our desks were arranged in groups of four facing each other. I liked that setup rather than everyone facing one direction, because it felt less like a classroom."

"I remember you used to always give us riddles and if/when we got the answers as a class, you would attach paper clips coming down from the top to the bottom of the whiteboard. If/when we hit the bottom, you'd bless us with a pizza party!"

"You had a fun spirit and rewarded us by playing games like Heads Up, Seven Up."

"My fondest and strongest memories are when you read Harry Potter and By the Great Horn Spoon aloud. It was something I looked forward to. I think those experiences really started my love for reading that's continued to this day."

I was right. Not a single one of their memories referenced a particular lesson. It was the little things that stood out in their minds. What about you? What do you remember about your favorite teachers growing up? More importantly, what are your students going to remember about you?

You Scratch My Back, I'll Scratch Yours

When I think back to my most memorable teachers, the one that immediately comes to mind is my fourth-grade teacher, Mrs. Olson. Memories of being in her class give me warm fuzzies. I vividly remember what the classroom looked like and where I sat, but what I remember most is one of the little things.

After lunch each day, Mrs. Olson had all of us students come to the front of the room and sit on the carpet where she would read aloud to us. I don't remember any of the books she read, but what I do remember is how we sat. As students, we would always arrange ourselves in lines, cross-legged, one student in front of the other. These lines branched out from where Mrs. Olson sat, like spokes on a wheel, and while she read to us, we would scratch each other's backs. We got to scratch each other's backs — *in school*! Of course, students always wanted to be in the front of a line, because then you'd get your back scratched without having to scratch someone else's. One of worst things that could befall a fourth-grader in Mrs. Olson's class was to end up on the carpet in the back of a line. Kids in her class were never late to line up after lunch. Being late to line up meant you'd more than likely end up in the back of a line on the carpet, meaning your back wasn't getting scratched that day. To us nine-year-olds, there were few things worse than a day without a scratched back.

You know what I don't remember about Mrs. Olson's class? Any of the curriculum she taught us. Seriously, I can't remember any math lessons, not one, though they had to have been present each and every day. I don't recall learning a single thing about the California Missions, though I'm sure there were plenty of lessons on this topic, a cornerstone of California's fourth-grade social studies curriculum.

I have no doubt that Mrs. Olson was a strong teacher, but what sticks out in my mind nearly 40 years later is how she made me feel, how she made my classmates feel. We loved her, but not because her pedagogy was solid. We loved her because she saw the importance of the little things. She realized something as simple as allowing her students to scratch each other's backs could make her classroom a place that didn't feel like school, a place where students wanted to be. And we did want to be there. Oh, how we did! Thank you, Mrs. Olson, for exercising this important facet of your EduInfluence, for using things deemed small to create memories that are big.

When Pizza Isn't Just Pizza

As the lead learner of my school, one of my privileges is the opportunity to host Lunch with the

THE POWER OF THE LITTLE THINGS

Principal. Each month, teachers select a student from their class who has been excelling academically, demonstrating perseverance, showing great character, etc., and those students get to join me to dine on gourmet Little Caesars pizza. Did I say gourmet? I meant inexpensive, though, to young kids, Little Caesars is gourmet. It's a fun way for me to sit down and chat with students, praise them for working hard and connect with them in a more relaxed setting. Totally casual. Just students, our assistant principal, and me, shooting the breeze over pizza. This time is always enjoyable, but one particular Lunch with the Principal this past year really reminded me of the Power of the Little Things.

It had been a typical monthly gathering, scheduled during a busy day, and after students had finished their pizza and were dismissed back to class, I walked through the staff lounge where one of our first-grade teachers stopped me in my tracks by saying, "Hey, Brent. Colin was so excited to have lunch with you today! He even got a haircut yesterday to get ready."

"Wait. What?" I said. "He got a haircut for Lunch with the Principal?"

"Yep. That's what he and his mom told me," she said with a smile.

Wow! I couldn't believe what I had heard, but apparently, getting to eat a $6 pizza with me was a pretty big deal for this six-year-old, enough so that he wanted to get a haircut beforehand. That's the elementary equivalent of a high school girl getting her hair and nails done before the prom, right? I was totally blown away. I was incredibly humbled. And then I felt a bit ashamed.

See, at that moment, I realized that in the busyness of my schedule, I had overlooked the importance of this time with my students and been guilty of viewing it as just one of the many things on my "to do" list that day. While perhaps small in the grand scheme of things, this wasn't about pizza. It was an opportunity to connect with my students, a chance to talk about their pets at home, what they like to play at recess and what they hoped to get for Christmas. It was an opportunity to get to know those I serve and for them to get to know me. I was reminded that students don't necessarily have a dozen things on their calendar that have to get done. I was reminded that for them, I may be the ONE thing on their "to do" list, the one thing they're looking forward to that day. **You may be the one thing your students are looking forward to today.** Your actions, even the small, simple ones like smiling, may be the highlight of a student's day, the reason he or she gets up in the morning.

So if you find yourself thinking, *"It's just a smile," "It's just a high five,"* or *"It's just pizza,"* remember — that smile, high five or time spent over pizza may be making a student's day, week, or even month. That student may be telling his or her mom and dad about the experience or writing about it in a journal. Who knows? Your simple action may even lead to a haircut.

THE POWER OF THE LITTLE THINGS

Deskside Manner

Before we move on, I want to clarify that in no way am I downplaying the importance of the "big" things in education. Make no mistake, things like utilizing sound instructional strategies and providing students with formative feedback are essential to being a successful teacher. You can't be great without them. The purpose of this chapter is not to encourage teachers to ignore such things, but rather remind us there is so much more to teaching, to being an effective leader, than simply knowing your content.

Take the example of a doctor's bedside manner. Doctors can have all the degrees in the world, know their particular branch of medicine like the back of their hand, but if they don't have good bedside manner, they probably won't have a lot of patients looking forward to their visits. Bedside manner, when compared to the knowledge and skills required in an area of medicine, could be considered to be secondary, to be a little thing. But is it? Yes, we want our doctors to have the "big" things down. We want them to know their stuff. But don't we also want them to have the "little" things like bedside manner?

I'm sure a lot of you are thinking that bedside manner isn't little, that's it's totally important. I completely agree, but if we had to choose between a heart surgeon's ability to perform open-heart surgery and his bedside manner, we'd probably take a great surgeon who isn't necessarily a people person. That being said, why can't we have both? Don't we as patients deserve both? Applying this example to education, if we are the doctors and our students are the patients, don't they deserve both?

My eye doctor totally gets this. This may sound crazy, but I actually look forward to my annual eye exam. As someone who has worn glasses and/or contact lenses since the beginning of fourth grade, I've had a lot of eye examinations in my life. But never had I looked forward to a checkup until I began seeing my current doctor. Why? Because my doctor recognizes the Power of the Little Things. His bedside manner is incredible! He is kind, personable, and he makes me feel like I give the correct answers to all his questions — questions that don't *have* right or wrong answers.

For those of you who aren't familiar with a visit to the eye doctor, here's how it works. You sit in the chair and look through what's called a phoropter, a weird-looking machine containing a whole bunch of interchangeable lenses. In order to determine your prescription, the doctor goes through a series of questions I call "Which looks better?" For each eye, the doctor has you look through two different lenses in the phoropter, asking you which lens gives you clearer vision. Depending on your answer, the doctor changes the lenses and again asks which one makes things clearer. He continues this process until he finds the perfect lens combination for you.

Here's how the conversation sounds with my doctor:

> *Doctor: "OK, which do you like better? Lens 1 or 2?"*

THE POWER OF THE LITTLE THINGS

Me: "1."
Doctor: "Good. Now if I change it to this, which is better? 1 or 2?"
Me: "Ummm....2."
Doctor: "Good. Good. How about this? 1 or 2?"
Me: "Still 2."
Doctor: "Good! Now, if I change this here, is it clearer or just a little smaller?"
Me: "Smaller."
Doctor: "Good! Good! OK, great job! That's it. Things look good!"

My doctor asks me a question, I give him an answer, and he says, "Good job!" Remember, there is no correct answer to any of these questions. I'm simply answering based on what my eyes tell me looks good. Yet my doctor praises me, and each time he does, I feel a little prouder about myself. I think, "Alright! I'm acing this test!"

I can't tell you how many times I have referred my eye doctor to friends. Do I refer him because of the degrees hanging on the wall in his office, the "big" things? Nope. Does it matter that he has those degrees, that he knows his stuff? Absolutely. He wouldn't be my doctor without having that training and expertise. But what sets him apart from every other eye doctor I've seen is the fact that he embraces the non-medical aspect of his job, what I'm sure some in his field might consider to be a minor thing. But he gets it. He wouldn't be my doctor if he didn't. See the connection here? **The best doctors have a wonderful bedside manner,**

and the best teachers have excellent "deskside" manner.

It's important to point out that the little things don't matter solely to kids. Remember Dr. Guillaume from Chapter 2, my graduate professor who made a huge impact on me by building relationships with her students? You know what else I remember her for? Putting smelly stickers on my tests. That's right, she put smelly stickers on students' exams when they did well. On the exams of *adults*, of graduate students. She chose to spend a few bucks at the teacher supply store to purchase smelly stickers, something typically reserved for elementary school students. The result? My classmates and I loved it! That small act of placing a fruit-, popcorn-, or pizza-scented sticker on our tests turned a room full of adults into giddy school-aged children. *"What kind did you get? Apple? I got bubble gum!"* On days when exams were set to be returned, I remember quietly hoping I had done well enough to earn a sticker. Let that sink in for a moment. A grown man in his early 30s was longing for a sticker, a *sticker*! The little things matter, even for adults.

In what ways are you leveraging the Power of the Little Things in your classroom or school? What small actions are making learning memorable for your students? Maybe you, like so many teachers, play instrumental music in your class to provide a calm and peaceful ambiance. If so, don't underestimate the impact this is having on your students.

When I taught fourth grade in the late '90s, I sometimes played a CD of Celtic music while students worked. I remember how one of my students, John, absolutely loved that CD. I remember that he particularly liked Track 3, so much so that whenever that one song would come on, he would get up from his desk and stand in front of my boombox, mesmerized by the tune emanating from the speakers. I can vividly picture him standing in front of the stereo, eyes closed, arms at his side, letting the music wash over him. Background music. A little thing, yet more than 20 years later, I can clearly remember the influence it had on John.

The little things matter, usually more than we realize. When things don't go as planned, when your lesson bombs, or you're feeling like you're not making a difference, don't let yourself be fooled. You're making more of an impact than you think. Remember the power contained in your simple actions, your deskside manner. Smiling. High-fiving students as they enter campus or the classroom. Complimenting them on their outfits. Asking about their weekend, and then giving your undivided attention as they tell you about it. These acts can make a student feel valued, feel loved, something far more important than a perfectly executed lesson.

As my PLN and former students showed, it's probably not the curriculum your students are going to remember. It's you. In a society that tells us to go big or go home, may this chapter serve as a reminder that bigger isn't always better.

STORIES OF EDUINFLUENCE

Belief to Embrace:

Sometimes the little things make the biggest impact.

Questions for Reflection:

- Think back to your favorite teachers growing up. What do you remember about them? Is it curriculum-related or the little things?
- How is your deskside manner? What little things do you do that help your students feel valued? If you're not sure, ask them.
- What could you do to improve your deskside manner? What's holding you back?

Tweet your thoughts and stories!
#EduInfluence

Chapter 9
The Power of Fun

> *"If you're not having fun,
> you're doing something wrong."*
> — *Groucho Marx*

"Why so serious?"

You may recall this famous line delivered by the late Heath Ledger as he masterfully portrayed the Joker in 2008's movie The Dark Knight. Ledger was magnificent in the role, and while this film is probably not the first to come to mind if asked to compile a list of inspirational movies for educators, I think the Joker's three-word question can serve as a great source of reflection for us as educators. That's right, we can learn something from a Batman movie. Bet you didn't expect that when you picked up this book, but stay with me. See, I believe that if we were able to read our students' minds, I think we'd find that many of them often ask themselves this question when they're in school — why so serious?

Unfortunately, I think there are some in education who still subscribe to the notion that school is an institution of learning and learning is serious business. Kids don't go to school to have fun, they go to school to learn. Ever heard this? I have and frankly put, you'll find 10 times more truth in a supermarket tabloid. Going back to the last chapter and the concept of bedside manner, why do we have to choose between a doctor who knows his or her stuff and one with good bedside manner? Why can't we have both? In the same way, why does school have to be a place of either learning or fun? Why can't students (and teachers) have both?

Kids want learning to be fun. Adults want learning to be fun. How many trainings or staff meetings have you sat through that didn't have enough fun infused into them, causing you to ask yourself, "Why so serious?" Shoot, how many staff meetings have I led that caused my teachers to ask themselves this question? More than one, that's for sure. Ouch! I'm writing this chapter for myself as much as for anyone.

Fun often starts with a smile, which reminds me of a teacher whom my daughter, Meghan, once had.

"My teacher never smiles," Meghan told my wife and me one evening about a month into that school year.

Wow! One month of school and not a single smile observed. Fast forward about six months. Meghan again came home from school, this time excited to tell us, "I made my teacher smile today!" She then proceeded to share the story of how a simple, humorous comment cracked the ever-serious countenance of her teacher, producing a smile. Meghan acted as if she'd witnessed the most elusive thing on the planet, like she'd seen Bigfoot. Yet it was just a smile, something that should be omnipresent in schools, not hard to find.

The purpose of sharing this story is not to bash or criticize this teacher. From what I knew, she was a very nice person who was instructionally solid. My daughter learned a lot that year and performed well in the class. But her teacher's lack of smiling was perceived by Meghan to be a lack of joy, a lack of having fun in what she was doing. As I wrote in Chapter 3, our example is powerful. Our students notice everything we do, even how much we smile. Kids want to see the adults around them having fun, because fun is contagious. What about you? Are you having fun doing what you do? If so, can your students tell? Can they see it on your face?

Laughter is the Best Medicine

Have you ever watched a stand-up comedian perform? Yes, I'm sure you've seen a comedy special on TV or watched a famous stand-up on YouTube, but have you ever seen a live comedy show? My wife and I had the pleasure of seeing Tim Hawkins perform live a few years ago, a show that made us laugh for two-and-a-half hours. If you're not familiar with this comic and like hilarious, family-friendly comedy, take a moment and look him up on YouTube (start by searching "Chick-fil-A Song"). Just finish this chapter first.

When the show was over, guess what my wife and I did pretty much the entire drive home? That's right, we talked about the show, retelling our favorite jokes, reliving the joy and laughter we had just experienced.

THE POWER OF FUN

Ever been to a funny movie and then quoted the funny lines or scenes on the way home, laughing all over again? It's what we do. Laughter has been scientifically proven to be good for us, so when we experience the gift that is a good laugh, we want that feeling to last.

See the connection to the classroom? I'm not saying we have to take the stage at the Improv to hone our comedic timing, but why can't our classrooms provide our students with the laughter and fun we so often seek for ourselves in television shows and movies? If we can make the classroom a fun place to be, a place of laughter, our students will leave school talking about it. Isn't that what we want?

I love to have fun with my students. Yes, when I was in the classroom, I held high expectations for student behavior and ran a structured room, but I also recognized the importance of making students laugh. I thought that if I could make learning experiences funny, students would go home talking about them. And just as importantly, they'd want to come back the next day for more.

When I taught fifth grade, I created one of those experiences, and it wasn't even planned. I was frontloading students with a few vocabulary words from the novel we were reading, and one of the terms was the word *spunky*. Spunky means full of spirit, which made me think of a cheerleader. They're spunky, right? Now, I could have just told my students that cheerleaders are spunky. I could have had my class draw a picture of a cheerleader to help them remember the definition of spunky. Or, I could have *shown* them what spunky looks like. Like I said, I wasn't planning on doing it, but at the moment, I saw an opportunity to make learning memorable. I saw an opportunity to make my students laugh, something that makes learning stick. I also saw an opportunity to pull a muscle. That's right, at that moment, I decided to break out into a cheerleading routine.

After providing them with the word's definition, I said to my students, "A cheerleader is an example of someone who is spunky. You've all seen cheerleaders, right? They look like this." And then I launched into probably the worst cheerleading routine of all time (my apologies to all you former cheerleaders out there). I snapped both my arms straight by my side and tucked my chin into my neck. With my head down, face toward the floor, I cried out, "Ready! Okay!" My head then popped up, and I began cheering.

"*We've got spirit, yes we do!*
We've got spirit, how 'bout you?
Mr. Coley's not a monkey!
He's just really, really spunky!
Yeah! Woo hoo! Woo hoo!"

While cheering, I flailed my arms about while holding invisible pom poms. I *tried* to do the jumping thing where you kick up one leg and clap your hands under that leg. Can you visualize it? On second thought, maybe that's not a good idea. I don't want to make anyone nauseous. I took every cheerleading stereotype and tried to do it. Again, my apologies to all the cheerleaders out there. It wasn't pretty.

My students' reaction? Complete silence for about two or three seconds. They were too shocked to speak, their mouths agape after what they had just witnessed. Then they lost it. Kids were falling out of their chairs, hysterical laughter coming from nearly every single student. Even the shy, reserved ones were laughing. I had tried to do something funny, to make them laugh so they'd remember the definition of a vocabulary word. Did it work? Uh, yeah. When it came time for the quiz, every single student knew what *spunky* meant. *Every single one*. But more than that, they went home that night and told their parents what had happened. I know, because parents came up to me afterward asking, "So, what's this Spunky Dance I'm hearing about?" Kids were talking about that moment for the rest of the year. Lasting memories had been created. Mission accomplished.

I recently got a nice surprise when two of my former students, sisters I taught in consecutive years nearly 10 years ago, dropped by my school to say hello. You know what they mentioned as we talked? That's right — the Spunky Dance. I did that dance every year after that first time to introduce students to spunky's definition, with the same positive results. Learning doesn't have to be boring. Having fun in class matters.

Deal or No Deal

Incorporating games into the classroom is a great and easy way to make learning fun. It could be something simple like letting students practice their multiplication facts using a deck of cards to play Multiplication War, a spin on the card game we grew up with, only students turn over two cards each, multiply them together, and the larger product wins. Online game-based platforms like Kahoot! or Quizizz are other great ways to introduce or review content in a way that engages students, rather than putting them to sleep. Whatever form it takes, be it an old-school deck of cards or new-school technology, games can be fun. And if students have fun, they are more likely to learn.

One of my good friends and fellow educator, Matt Stricker (@coachstricker), is a huge Denver Broncos fan. When he taught sixth grade, he decided to take his love for his favorite team and turn it into a game for his students in an attempt to create some fun. Matt came up with something he called "John Elway Trivia," and every Monday he would post a trivia question about the Broncos Hall-of-Fame quarterback. He would give his students until Friday to find and submit their answers and then, before dismissing them for the weekend, Matt would randomly select one of the answer submissions. If the answer was correct *and* that student had completed all of his or her work on time that week, Matt would reward the student with a small prize.

When Matt shared with me this simple idea, I thought it was a terrific way to inject a little fun into class while reinforcing the importance of responsibility. Did John Elway have anything to do with the curriculum or sixth-grade content standards?

THE POWER OF FUN

Nope, but that didn't matter. What mattered was the fact that Matt's students got excited each week to see if they could win a prize. His students enjoyed it. It was fun. That's what mattered.

I decided to try something similar in my classroom, though my game was called The Weekly Homophone Challenge. Each Monday, I posted a different homophone riddle on a small bulletin board by the classroom door. For example, students would walk into the room and see a question like this affixed to the board:

"What do you call an undecorated flying machine?"

Next to the bulletin board was a small coffee mug filled with blank slips of paper on which students could write their answers. Next to the coffee mug was an empty coffee can with a slit cut into the plastic top into which students could drop their answers. Remember those pre-Keurig days, when coffee came in cans of pre-ground coffee beans that actually had to be placed in a filter before brewing? Oh, what coffee drinkers had to endure before the invention of K-Cups! But while this may have made for a little more work for our morning coffee, those old coffee cans were gold in the classroom! As it was in Matt's room, my students had all week to figure out the answer to that week's riddle. In case you're wondering, an undecorated flying machine is a *plain plane*.

On Friday afternoons, I would randomly select an answer, and if it was correct and the student had completed all work on time that week, he or she would win not a prize, but an opportunity to play *Deal or No Deal*. Remember the popular game show from the mid- to late-2000's hosted by Howie Mandel and recently resurrected on CNBC? If not, the concept was very straightforward. No trivia questions to answer. No special skills required. A contestant selected one of 26 briefcases, each containing a dollar amount ranging from $.01 to $1,000,000. The contestant then chose to open, one at a time, the remaining numbered briefcases to reveal the dollar amounts they contained, hoping to open cases with small amounts (for by revealing small amounts, that meant there was a better chance of a large amount being in the contestant's case). Periodically, the "banker" would offer the contestant a sum of money to buy his or her case. Howie Mandel would then dramatically ask the contestant, "Deal ... or no deal?" — take the banker's offer, or continue to open cases in hopes of winning more money.

Each week's winner of The Weekly Homophone Challenge got to play a computerized version of the game I had on my classroom computer that was displayed through an LCD projector for the class to see. Students didn't play for money, but rather pieces of licorice. Using the conversion chart below, students had a chance to win as many as 100 pieces of licorice, pretty much the equivalent of winning a million dollars for a 10-year-old.

THE POWER OF FUN

Deal or No Deal Conversion Chart	
$.01 - $49,999	1 piece
$50,000 - $99,999	3 pieces
$100,000 - $149,999	5 pieces
$150,000 - $199,999	6 pieces
$200,000 - $249,999	7 pieces
$250,000 - $299,999	8 pieces
$300,000 - $349,999	9 pieces
$350,000 - $399,999	10 pieces
$400,000 - $449,999	11 pieces
$450,000 - $499,999	12 pieces
$500,000 - $749,999	15 pieces
$750,000 - $999,999	20 pieces
$1,000,000	100 pieces

Each and every Friday I would play the role of Howie Mandel, asking that week's lucky contestant, "Deal or no deal?" I got into game-show-host character, my goal to work the class into a frenzy, to build the drama with each case that was opened. Every time I asked that question, students would go crazy, some screaming, "Take the deal!" while others pleaded with their classmate to go on — "No deal! No deal! No deal!" Anyone walking by my classroom at that time would have wondered what in the world was going on. The answer? Fun. That's what was going on. By carving out about 10 minutes once a week — 10 measly minutes —

I created fun, and not just for my students. I looked forward to this weekly time. I loved seeing the excitement on students' faces as they willed their friends to win it all. I sent students home for the weekend with something to talk about, and on three occasions over the years, a student went home with 100 pieces of licorice.

The bottom line is this — **in an age of standards and accountability, we cannot abandon fun in the name of learning. The two are not mutually exclusive.** Learning can be fun. Learning *should* be fun. I'm also not saying we should abandon the standards and just play games all day. What I'm saying is students and teachers can have both. Our students deserve both. We deserve both. Not comfortable with busting out a cheerleading routine? That's fine. Do whatever you are comfortable with that will make your classroom or school a fun place where students want to be. Maybe that means incorporating a weekly game like The Weekly Homophone Challenge. Maybe it means using online tools like Kahoot! to gamify a lesson. Maybe it means just being silly with students once in a while or periodically telling a joke. Maybe it's as simple as consciously smiling more.

Have fun! Make it part of your daily routine. Your students will thank you and, just as importantly, you'll thank yourself.

THE POWER OF FUN

Belief to Embrace:

We cannot abandon fun in the name of learning. The two are not mutually exclusive.

Questions for Reflection:

- Which of your teachers growing up made learning the most fun for you? How so?
- What do you do to make learning fun in your classroom or school?
- On a scale from 1-10 (with 10 being the highest), how do you think your students would rate the level of fun in your class?
- What could you do to make your class more fun for your students?

Tweet your thoughts and stories!
#EduInfluence

Chapter 10
The Power of Conviction

*"When you do the right things in the right way,
you have nothing to lose because
you have nothing to fear."*
— Zig Ziglar

Mistakes.

Failure.

Years ago, these two words would have been viewed by many with disdain, as something to avoid like the plague. Yet in today's classrooms, these two words and the potential they possess are often viewed in a positive light, even celebrated. Why? Because we know that a mistake isn't the end of the road. We know that failure doesn't have to be fatal. So we make it a point to encourage our students to take risks, to not give up when things get tough. We encourage them to build their perseverance, reminding them that with productive struggle comes growth. We teach them about Carol Dweck's research and the concept of growth mindset, that intelligence is not fixed, that they can get smarter by practicing something they're not yet

THE POWER OF CONVICTION

good at. We teach our students the power of "yet," as in "I'm not able to do this *yet*."

But how often do we as educators practice what we preach? How often do we embrace our mistakes, celebrate our failures? How often do we think of trying something new, something we know would benefit our students, but don't because we're afraid it might not work? How often do we go with what's comfortable, simply because it's easy? How often do we rely on what's worked in the past, rather than stepping out of our comfort zone to be even better for kids? I've certainly been guilty of it, and I think if we're honest with ourselves, we all have.

In this chapter though, I want to take this idea a step further. How often do we choose not to follow our hearts in the classroom because we're afraid it might be frowned upon by those around us? How often do we play it safe because of what the principal might think? How often do we not do what we *know* is right, because we're afraid it might *look* wrong? That's the Power of Conviction — following your heart, doing what's best for kids, even though it may buck the system or look "wrong" in some people's eyes.

In the pages that follow, I'm going to share two personal stories, one from early in my teaching career and one from my transition from the classroom to administration. We all have moments when we must make a decision — do what *looks* right, or do what *is* right. It's not always easy, but exercising this component of our EduInfluence is critical if we are to pursue excellence for our students and ourselves.

STORIES OF EDUINFLUENCE

What's He Gonna Do?

Have you ever had one of those moments in your career when someone walks into your classroom at just the right time? Maybe your principal walked into the room right when your students were in small groups, fully engaged in analytic conversations about the book they were reading. Or perhaps the superintendent stopped by for a visit during a Number Talk, and your students were blowing you away with their explanations of the various mental strategies they were using to solve a math problem, clearly demonstrating a solid conceptual understanding. You know, those moments that make you want to break out a huge fist pump and utter, "Yes!" under your breath. That is such a good feeling!

Now, how about the opposite? Ever had a visitor show up at just the wrong time? You know what I'm talking about. That time when your lesson is not going as planned, kids are off task, and "Johnny" is having a rough day behaviorally. That moment the door opens, your principal walks in, and you think to yourself, *"Seriously? Now? Why couldn't you have come in this morning, or even 10 minutes ago?"* We've all been there.

Back in the early stages of my teaching career, I had one of those moments. I was teaching fifth grade and had a class of students that was, shall we say, challenging. Can you relate? Sweet kids, but wow! They pushed the limits nearly every single day. In my 15 years as a classroom teacher, this was my most challenging group.

One of the things they particularly struggled with was talking at inappropriate times, especially during transitions. As I've previously written, I liked to run a structured classroom, a tight ship, so you can imagine how this unnecessary talking went over with me. See, it wasn't about wanting a quiet classroom. It was about maximizing instructional time. There was barely enough time in the day to get through everything we needed to cover, so wasting time trying to get students back on task as they transitioned from one lesson to another didn't sit well with me.

What made it worse was the fact that students were choosing to do it. They were clearly capable of quickly taking out a math book without carrying on a conversation with a neighbor. They had done it when they wanted to, but time and time again (and again and again) they chose to demonstrate that this wasn't a priority for them. They didn't respond to positive incentives and, believe me, I implemented a bunch of them. Warnings bounced off students like bullets to Superman's chest. Small consequences didn't deter the negative behavior, either. I tried every trick in my bag. Nothing worked. Have you been there? Maybe you're there right now.

So one day, well into the second semester, after multiple poor transitions and a mental calculation of the time that was being wasted, I stepped it up. I decided to go Old School.

STORIES OF EDUINFLUENCE

"Boys and girls," I said slowly, "I have reminded you over and over again what is expected when you're asked to get something out of your desks. Yet over and over again you continue to choose to talk, making transitions longer and wasting precious class time. I'm sorry, guys, but if it happens again, we're going to have to practice transitioning without talking. We're going to practice taking our books out of our desks. We're going to do it 20 times, and the time it takes to practice this will be taken off of your recess."

Now, before we move on, let me acknowledge that this classroom management strategy is not the foundation upon which great classrooms are built. You're not going to find this approach on many Pinterest boards. I fully get that. I don't believe punitive approaches are the best way to deal with student misbehavior. But this is where I was, a fairly new teacher searching for a solution. My students were seemingly immune to every other strategy I had tried. Things were disintegrating in my room, so I was ready to give Old School a shot.

So back to the story. A final warning had been extended. Surely this would work.

Uh, no. The very next time they were asked to transition quietly, they did the exact same thing. They immediately turned to classmates and began talking. It was like they were daring me to do something about it. So I did.

"OK, that's it," I firmly said. "Eyes and ears on me." I waited until every single pair of eyes was fixed on mine, which now held a dead-serious look. "Boys and

THE POWER OF CONVICTION

girls, apparently you didn't think I was serious. Well, I am. When I say, 'Go,' please take out your math book. If you choose to talk, you will receive a citation (a school-wide method of documenting negative behavior — something students did *not* want to get). Do you all understand?" Every student nodded, a look of *"Oh, man. He's not messing around"* on their faces.

"Go," I said.

Students quietly pulled out their books and put them on their desks.

"Good. Now, when I say, 'Go,' without a word, please put them back in your desks. Go."

Students perfectly executed the request, quietly placing their books back in their desks.

"Good. That's one," I said. "Only 19 more to go."

Out. In. Out. In. Out. In. You could have heard a pin drop. Old School in full effect.

Here's where the story takes a turn. When we were about halfway to 20, the handle on the classroom door turned, and the door slowly swung open. Want to guess who walked in? That's right. The principal. Dr. Dameron, our amazing administrator, walked into the back of the room smiling, and I'll never forget what happened next.

Bailey, the same student from Chapter 3 and the water bottle story, turned her head toward the door and saw Dr. Dameron enter. Bailey then swiveled her head back toward me, then back to the principal, then back to me, a concerned look on her face. Her expression communicated, *"Oh, no! Mr. Coley, you're going to get in trouble! What are you gonna do?"* She looked genuinely concerned for me. I was touched.

So what did I do?

I smiled at Bailey and attempted to give her a compassionate look that conveyed, *"Thank you for your concern, but we're not done."*

"When I say, 'Go,'" I continued as I smiled at Bailey, "please put your books away. Go." I continued for one more "In, Out" rotation and then turned to our principal.

"Hi, Dr. Dameron. Unfortunately, my class has really been having a hard time transitioning without talking. I've tried positive incentives, warnings, small consequences, but they've continued to choose to talk and waste instructional time. I told them that if they continued to make the choice to talk, we'd have to practice taking books out quietly and take that time off their recess. That's what we're doing right now."

And there it was. The principal had walked into the room as I was disciplining the class. Definitely not the ideal time for a visit. How would she respond?

Dr. Dameron folded her arms across her chest, looked down and shook her head.

"Uh, oh," I thought. *"She's shaking her head."*

Dr. Dameron remained silent, her head down.

"Oh, man. This isn't good."

After what seemed like an eternity, but in reality, was probably only two or three seconds, Dr. Dameron looked up at the class. She shook her head, a look of disappointment on her face. She then turned back to me, nodded, and gave me an approving thumbs-up.

THE POWER OF CONVICTION

"Carry on, Mr. Coley," she said and walked out of the room, giving the class a final raised eyebrow and look of admonishment before she left.

I'd be lying if I said I didn't exhale in relief after she'd gone. But with a confidence beyond my years of experience, I had exercised my Power of Conviction, long before I even realized I possessed it. What I was doing might have looked wrong to an outside observer. The principal walked in as I was having my students take books out of their desks over and over and over again. At first glance (and perhaps second and third glance as well), that didn't look good, didn't look like teaching. But it was. While I may have used an unconventional approach, one I don't believe should be our "go-to" strategy, I was teaching my students to be respectful and responsible with their time (as well as with mine). Looking back, do I think this was the perfect way to handle the situation? Probably not. Were there other strategies I could have tried? Probably. But there was a purpose to what I chose to do, a purpose that on the surface wasn't necessarily visible. Had I given in to the fear that what I was doing looked wrong and stopped holding students accountable as soon as the principal walked in, who knows how things would have progressed in the class. But I didn't. I believed in what I was doing, stood my ground, and things dramatically changed for the better for the remainder of the school year.

Things you do in your classroom aren't always going to look like how others think they should. But if you're taking a risk to be better for kids, if you're putting students' interests at the heart of what you're doing, don't ever let the fear of an outside opinion stop you from following your heart.

What's the Desire of Your Heart?

As I wrote in the introduction, I never had any aspirations of going into administration. But over the years, I was nudged by the principals I worked under to pursue an administrative credential to open potential career doors down the road.

In the fall of 2005, I decided to return to school to start coursework toward earning an administrative credential. In May of 2007, I finished the program and was certified to move into a site leadership position. Mind you, I was in no rush to leave the classroom. I absolutely loved what I was doing. Plus, at that time the budget situation in California was extremely bleak. I didn't see any new positions opening up, and I certainly didn't anticipate any new ones being created. And that was fine. I was content to remain in Room 34 at Tovashal Elementary School with my 32 fifth-graders until God saw fit to open a door for a new opportunity. Little did I know that opportunity would come knocking just a few months later.

In November of that year, my principal called me into her office and let me know she was going to need to have surgery over winter break and would be out for about three months to recover. While she was out, our assistant principal would serve as acting principal, and my principal wanted to know if I was interested in coming out of the classroom for those three months to serve as acting assistant principal. She knew that I had recently earned my administrative credential and thought it would be a great way for me to gain some experience in an administrative capacity. I was thrilled with the prospect of gaining some on-the-job training in an environment in which I was already comfortable, so I said I would be honored to help out.

As we neared winter break, my principal thought it would be a good idea to begin the transition a little early, so rather than wait until returning to school in January, I moved up to the office a week before the break. This gave me five days to settle in so that when we returned in January, I could hit the ground running (or at least stumbling, as was more likely the case for a newbie like me).

Unfortunately, this is where the story takes a heartbreaking turn. Due to post-surgery complications, my principal tragically passed away, never making it out of the hospital. Our school community was devastated. We had lost our beloved leader and now had to pick up the pieces. As difficult as it was, the acting principal and I were tasked to lead the school forward amid the most trying of circumstances.

In an effort to maintain as much consistency for the site as possible, district leadership asked me to finish out the school year in the position, and I immediately agreed to do so. What was planned as three months of slowly wading into the administrative pool became, out of necessity, what felt like being thrown into the deep end. Understand, the outpouring of support offered by district leadership and support staff was tremendous, more than I could have hoped for. But it was difficult. Very difficult. Losing a staff member at any time is devastating. Losing your leader mid-year is on another level. It was probably the most challenging six months of my career. At the same time, I would be hard-pressed to identify another six-month period where I grew more. Through suffering comes strength, and though exhausted and a bit bruised, I came out on the other side a better educator.

As the year wound down, I expressed to district leadership that if they saw me as a good fit, I was interested in continuing in the role of assistant principal. Not long after that, I heard from the district that they did want to keep me in the position for the following year. I remember getting off the phone and letting out a huge "Yes!" in my car. And then as if a switch had been flipped, my joy turned into doubt, and I began to question myself.

"Do I really want this? Am I sure I'm ready to leave the classroom?"

It was crazy. I had worked so hard over the past two-and-a-half years to give myself this opportunity. Now the opportunity was about to be placed before me, and I wasn't sure if I wanted it. What was I supposed to do?

As I have done so often over the years when I've needed wisdom, I called my dad. He came over that night, and I explained the situation I was wrestling

THE POWER OF CONVICTION

with. I was so conflicted, not knowing what to do. I was excited about the chance to become an assistant principal, but I wasn't sure if I was ready to leave the classroom. If I declined an opportunity like this, would I be letting people down? Would I be committing career suicide? I talked. My dad listened. We prayed. After an hour-and-a-half, I was still torn. And then my dad patiently looked at me and asked one simple question.

"Brent, what's the desire of your heart?"

Such a simple question, yet it cut through everything else. All the doubt vanished, and the floodgates opened.

"To go back to the classroom," I replied, breaking down in sobs of relief. The classroom. That was the desire of my heart and simply saying it out loud gave me peace. I knew it was the right decision.

Then came the hard part — telling district leadership and my staff. Was there a fear my choice would hinder any future career advancement? Yes, but I knew I was making the right decision. I had to follow my heart. God would take care of my future. Was there fear I'd be letting my staff down? Yep. But I couldn't make my decision based on fear.

So, did it all work out? Better than I could have imagined. District leadership was incredibly understanding. In fact, I was told I garnered more respect in their eyes because I followed my heart. My staff was supportive as well, and I returned to the classroom for three more years. Someone once told me years later that I needed to go back to the classroom because approximately 100 students needed me to be their teacher and I needed them to be my students. I believe this wholeheartedly. I was exactly where I needed to be at exactly the right time.

That's the Power of Conviction — doing what's right, even when it may look wrong in someone else's eyes, or when someone expects you to do something different.

So what does this mean for you? If you're a teacher, it means not listening to that little voice in your head that discourages you from trying something new with your students, because it might not look like "teaching." In the movie *Dead Poets Society*, teacher John Keating didn't care what it looked like when he and his students stood on his desk to demonstrate the need to look at things differently. Could that have looked bad if the headmaster had walked in? Sure, but Keating wasn't worried about what it looked like. His only concern was making Shakespeare come alive for the young men in his class. Doing things the conventional way is safe. But limiting ourselves to conventional thinking will never lead to new ways to engage students. Remember my Spunky Dance from the previous chapter? How would that have looked if my principal had walked in during my spastic routine? Would have raised an eyebrow, I'm sure, but I didn't care. It wasn't about what it looked like. It was about creating a learning experience that would be remembered. **The bottom line is this — if it's good for kids, go for it!**

THE POWER OF CONVICTION

If you're a site administrator, you have a critical role in developing the Power of Conviction in your teachers. Remember, I'm a site principal, so I'm preaching what I need to hear. If we want our teachers to take risks in the classroom, we have to make it safe for them to do so. We can tell classroom teachers until we're blue in the face that we want them to step out of their comfort zones to better engage their students, but if our actions don't create an environment where they feel secure to do so, our words are meaningless, and that risk-taking just isn't going to happen. If we pop into a classroom to see a teacher doing something like standing on his desk, rapping the lyrics to a states and capitals song to a classful of mesmerized, smiling students, that needs to be celebrated. And if we happen to enter a room and observe a teacher taking a risk that isn't going as planned, maybe even bombing, that needs to be celebrated as well (perhaps even more). A teacher who receives no encouragement after a less-than-successful attempt at something new is a teacher likely to go right back to the safety of the filing cabinet containing drawers full of "these have worked in the past" lessons. It is our responsibility to foster an environment where teachers can follow their hearts to do what's best for students, even if that looks unconventional or doesn't work the first time.

Follow your heart, because if the best interests of students are in your heart, you can't lose. In the words of Pamela Wilson (@strengthpeace), a retired teacher, administrator, and assistant superintendent, "If we're

STORIES OF EDUINFLUENCE

doing what's best for kids, no one can question our decision making."

THE POWER OF CONVICTION

Belief to Embrace:

Doing the right thing may look wrong in some people's eyes.

Questions for Reflection:

- Have you ever had someone walk into your classroom at the wrong time, when things weren't going as planned? What were the circumstances?
- When is a time you tried something in your classroom that could have looked "wrong" to an outside observer?
- Have you ever wanted to take a risk but didn't for fear of how it may have been perceived? What was it you wanted to do?

Tweet your thoughts and stories!
#EduInfluence

Chapter 11
The Power of the Extra Mile
(Bonus Chapter)

> *"Never worry about numbers. Help one person at a time and always start with the person nearest you."*
> — Mother Teresa

Teaching is difficult.

Not a revelation, is it? There are two categories into which we could place this statement: "Tell me something I don't know" or "Duh!"

It doesn't matter if you've been a teacher for 10 years or 10 days, you know that teaching is an extremely challenging profession. There is so much responsibility placed in our hands, the responsibility not just to build academic skills but also to help shape students' character. Also, education is one of the only professions where the long-standing, unwritten expectation is that teachers put in time outside of contractual hours. In most districts, teachers are not required to report back to work at the start of a new school year until just a few days before students return. Many teachers are greeted by empty classrooms, blank canvases, and are expected to transform those rooms into engaging learning spaces. Because this task is nearly impossible to complete in a day or two, most teachers come in early to get their rooms ready for students. They put in the extra time because they want the best for their kids. They do it because it's what needs to be done.

It's safe to say virtually every teacher puts in more time than is contractually obligated. In that sense, every teacher goes the extra mile (or at least the extra yards). What I want to talk about in the coming pages is the power that lies in going that extra mile, or even the extra, *extra* mile, even when those efforts go largely unnoticed. We don't do what we do for recognition. We don't put in the hard work for adulation or awards. But what happens when we go above and beyond, and it appears that extra work isn't making a difference? What happens when the only noticeable result from going the extra mile is sore feet? Is that extra work worth it? I'm here to tell you the answer is a resounding YES!

StudyCast

As I mentioned in Chapter 4, I created and maintained a classroom website during the majority of my 15 years in the classroom. My site was my baby, my labor of love. To say I spent a lot of time on it would be an understatement. I worked on it constantly. While some folks find enjoyment and relaxation by taking walks, gardening or reading, I loved to "work" on my website. I was always looking for that new thing to add to the site that could be a resource for my students, their parents, or other teachers. I spent a ton of time on the site. Just ask my patient wife.

Back in the mid-2000s, I came across an idea from Eric Langhorst (@ELanghorst), middle-school history teacher and 2008 Missouri Teacher of the Year. Eric was creating a podcast for his students where he recorded himself reviewing the content for upcoming tests or quizzes. He called it StudyCast. It was so simple — a short audio file his students could listen to on their time to help them study. It was pure genius. I knew I had to try this with my students. I reached out to Eric to ask permission to use the concept and name StudyCast with my own students, and he graciously agreed.

Soon, I was doing the same thing with my class, recording StudyCasts to help my own students review for tests in Social Studies, Science, and Language Arts. Before each test, I would grab my notes for the unit, sit in front of a microphone plugged into my computer, and simply talk about what was going to be covered on the test. The beauty of a StudyCast was that I was able to talk about anecdotes or stories

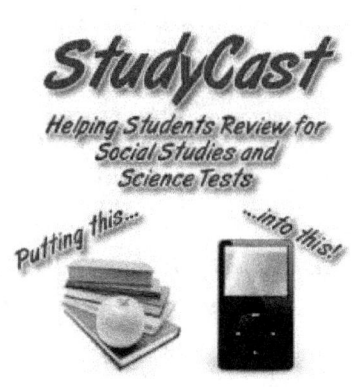

THE POWER OF THE EXTRA MILE

I told in class that weren't necessarily in students' notes, and students were able to listen on their computer or iPod (yes, an iPod, which tells you this was several years ago). Studying for a test didn't seem quite as bad when you could do so using an iPod. If you're interested in getting an idea of what a StudyCast sounded like, you can visit www.mrcoley.com/studycast to listen to the broadcasts I created during my final year in the classroom before moving into administration.

So naturally, every one of my students took advantage of this digital resource, right?

Wrong.

Unfortunately, while the majority of my students had listened to a StudyCast or two, very few in the class were what I considered to be regular listeners. Access wasn't an issue, as nearly every student had an Internet-connected computer at home, and a large number of kids had iPods or similar mobile media players.

To be honest, this was frustrating. I didn't want *some* students listening, I wanted *all* of them to listen, and I had a hard time understanding why more of them weren't utilizing this study tool. Can you relate? Ever gone above and beyond for your class, only to be disappointed because your efforts didn't seem to be paying the dividends you were expecting? I mean, I wasn't asking my students to crack open the textbook. I was giving them the chance to pop in earbuds or headphones and listen on the go, perhaps while sitting in the backseat of the car as their mom or dad drove around town running errands.

In an attempt to boost listenership, I even took to offering incentives to listening by inserting secret codes into broadcasts. When I recorded, sometimes midway through a broadcast I would stop and say something like, "OK, boys and girls. I want to stop for a moment and thank you for listening. The secret code word for this broadcast is 'watermelon.' The first person to email me the code word or tell me in class will receive three extra credit points on the test."

Surely this helped in giving students a reason to listen, right?

Nope. Not really. Sometimes I'd release a new StudyCast, and not a single student would tell me the secret code, letting me know no one had listened or didn't listen all the way through.

Again, this was disheartening. There were times when I asked myself, *"Why are you doing this, Brent? You're putting in all this time and effort to create these broadcasts, and only a few students, if that, are listening."* More than once I considered abandoning StudyCasts, telling myself it wasn't worth the time and effort I was putting in.

Then one day I was reminded of the Power of the Extra Mile.

In 2009, I learned I was going to have the opportunity to give my first presentation at a statewide educational technology conference. My session was called "Podcasts and iPod Flashcards: Study Tools for the 21st Century," and in it, I was planning to share

THE POWER OF THE EXTRA MILE

with other teachers the StudyCast concept. As I was preparing, I asked my students for some feedback on StudyCasts. I knew what *I* thought about this audio study aid. I thought it was the greatest thing since sliced bread. But what really mattered was what my students thought. So I asked them.

Here's what one student said:

> "When I study the StudyCast, I get a better grade, and it helps me study for big tests. It really works, and I love it!"

Yes! This was exactly what I needed to hear! For this student, StudyCasts were something she enjoyed using to help her study, and they appeared to be working. For her, my efforts had paid off. And if that wasn't good enough, I then came across this piece of student feedback:

> "I like the StudyCasts because I can listen to them on my computer while I'm doing my homework. I listened to the Puritan StudyCast five times, and I got a good grade."

Wait, how many times did she listen? Five times? This absolutely floored me. It's hard enough to get some students to study, to get them to review their notes even *one* time, yet this particular student listened to the StudyCast on one of our Social Studies units five times. *Five times!*

This was the reminder I needed, and in it lay the truth behind this facet of our EduInfluence — **going**

the extra mile is worth it, even if it only benefits a single student.

Did I want all of my students to use StudyCasts? Yes. Did they? No. And that's OK because, for at least these two students, my extra time and effort made a difference. If I had stopped creating these broadcasts because more students weren't leveraging this tool, I would have denied these two the additional support they needed. Who knows? StudyCasts may have been the only thing motivating these two to study.

One more recent story to illustrate this point. Every month I record a video message to my school community, which I then upload to YouTube and our school's website. I call the videos ColeyCasts, and in each broadcast, I discuss coming events and highlight the amazing things taking place on our campus. With a student population of nearly 900, each month's broadcast averages less than 100 views. Now, I could choose to be disappointed by the fact more people aren't watching, but instead, I choose to remember how the parent of one of our first-grade students recently let me know how much her son looks forward to watching each month's broadcast. She even sent me a picture of him sitting in front of their computer watching intently! A first-grader! If no one else watches, I know my efforts are making a difference in the life of this six-year-old, and that's reason enough to continue going the extra mile.

THE POWER OF THE EXTRA MILE

Personal Inspiration

The summer before her fourth-grade year, my daughter, Meghan, was enrolled at a new school in our district. While this change was going to substantially make things more manageable for my wife regarding drop-offs in the mornings and pick-ups in the afternoons, it also understandably created a bit of nervousness for Meghan. A new school meant having to make new friends, something that can be tough for many nine-year-olds. As the first day of school got closer and closer, Meghan's nervousness became greater and greater. My wife and I did our best to reassure her, reminding her that one of her good friends would be at the school with her, but unfortunately, our efforts weren't all that successful in allaying her worries. As parents, it was tough.

At that time I was also preparing for a new school year, which would end up being my last year teaching fifth grade before moving into administration. As I did each year, I came into my classroom well before I was required to report back to work so that I could organize desks, set up my reading corner and put up bulletin boards.

One day, as I was putting the finishing touches on my classroom setup, I recall thinking about Meghan. As her father, I remember wanting so desperately to take away all her fears of the unknown. I knew she was going to rock it at her new school. I knew that once she got there, she would be just fine, more than fine. But transferring that confidence to my nine-year-old wasn't quite so easy. I remember thinking to myself, *"If Meghan could just see her classroom. If she could just hear her teacher's voice ..."*

I looked around my classroom, an environment I had worked so hard to transform into a colorful, inviting space for my future students.

And then it hit me.

The light bulb went on.

I didn't have the ability to show Meghan her new classroom or let her hear her new teacher's voice, but I did have the power to make that happen for *my* students. What if one of my future pupils was feeling like Meghan, nervous about the unknown, maybe even having trouble sleeping because of worry? Through the magic of technology, I realized I possessed the power to lessen any potential anxiety in my students by showing them their new classroom, by letting them hear *my* voice.

I immediately grabbed my phone and called my dad, asking to borrow his Flip Video camera. Remember, at that time, cell phones didn't have the high-quality video cameras they do now, so a Flipcam was the next best thing. I told him what I wanted to do, drove over to his house that evening, and the next day was back in my classroom, video camera in hand. My goal was to create a "classroom tour" video that I would then upload to **mrcoley.com** for students to view.

Standing at the door of my classroom, I pointed the camera into the room and hit the "Record" button.

"Hey, boys and girls!" I said into the camera's microphone. "This is Mr. Coley, and if you're going to be in my class this year, I wanted to give you a little preview of what the classroom looks like. So, here it is …"

I then walked around the classroom, pointing the camera at various spots in the room, narrating as I went. The video ended up only being two or three minutes long. There was no script of what to say, and I did it in one take. No editing. If I coughed, I simply said, "Excuse me," and continued. See, the idea wasn't to create a polished work of art, but rather to give students a glimpse at what would be their school home for the next 180 days. The goal was to make them feel comfortable before they even stepped foot in the classroom. I uploaded the video to **mrcoley.com**, and when classroom lists were announced to families a few days later, students were encouraged to visit the site and watch the video. This was going to be great! This video was going to make a difference for each and every one of the 32 students on my roster!

On the first day of school, I asked students to raise their hands if they had watched the classroom tour video. I was so excited, anticipating a sea of hands shooting up.

Two. Two hands went up.

Once again, I was initially frustrated. Only *two* students watched the video? Why only two? I hadn't spent a ton of time to make the video, but I was hoping to reach more than a couple students. Fortunately, I quickly reminded myself that it didn't matter how many watched the video. I reminded myself of this truth — if even *one* student watched and slept more soundly the night before school started, the effort it took to make and publish the video was worth it. And I had reached *two* students!

What really drove the point home for me was this — one of those two students could have been Meghan. One of those two students could have been my daughter. What if her teacher had the idea to create a video like this, but then decided against it because she didn't think the whole class would watch it? What if her teacher was ready to go the extra mile but opted not to because she didn't think it was worth the effort for only one or two students?

The truth is this — it is absolutely worth the effort, even if that work only benefits a single student. Because that one student could be your son. That one student could be your daughter. When we put in the effort to provide something extra for our students, of course, we want to reach as many as possible. Please don't misunderstand my message. We should always strive to meet the needs of *all* our students. But if you're thinking of going above and beyond for your students even if you think it'll only benefit a few, do it!

Maybe you're thinking of creating a graphic organizer to help with a writing task. Will all of your students need it? Perhaps not, but if even one student could utilize that tool to help him or her be successful, isn't your effort worth it?

Maybe it's creating a class Instagram account to showcase the great things taking place in your classroom. Will it take some extra work to set up the account, take pictures, and post them? Yes. Will all of your students and their parents follow along? Probably not, but what if that online resource, that cherry on top, is the one thing that keeps one of your students engaged and wanting to come to school each day?

Or maybe you read about the idea of writing notes of encouragement to every student in your class and are considering doing so. Will it take time? Yes. Might some students think to themselves, *"That's nice,"* and toss the note in the trash? Maybe. But what about that one student who will keep that note all year, frequently going back to reread it, giving her a reason to get up in the morning? That note may be a lifeline for a student who is just hanging on.

When we go the extra mile for our students, we want to reach as many as we can. That's the heart of an educator. But never let the possibility of some students not taking advantage of your extra effort prevent you from going above and beyond. Isn't that what we want from our own children's teachers? Your extra effort is making a difference, even if it doesn't look like it. So lace up those metaphorical shoes and start walking or running that extra mile, even if there will only be one smiling student at the finish line to greet you.

STORIES OF EDUINFLUENCE

Belief to Embrace:

Going the extra mile is worth it,
even if it only benefits a single person.

Questions for Reflection:

- When is a time you went beyond the call of duty for your students, only to be disappointed that it didn't have as large an impact as you expected?
- Can you think of a time one of your teachers went above and beyond for you? What was the circumstance?
- What is one thing you could do to go the extra mile for your students?

Tweet your thoughts and stories!
#EduInfluence

Chapter 12
Unleash Your EduInfluence

> *"A teacher affects eternity; he can never tell where his influence stops."*
> — Henry Brooks Adams

Education is not the same as it was when I began teaching over 20 years ago. When I got the keys to my first classroom in 1996, the room had a chalkboard, no carpet, no Internet-connected computer, and a telephone without the capability of dialing an outside line. Today, the classrooms in my school are all equipped with ceiling-mounted LCD projectors, document cameras, voice-amplification systems, mobile devices, and the ability to connect with classrooms all over the world with just a few taps or clicks.

Technology provides the teachers of today tools to engage and meet the needs of students in ways never before possible. Google's G Suite for Education and Microsoft's Office 365 enable students to create stunning multimedia projects to demonstrate their learning, individually or in collaboration with someone on the other side of the room or the other side of the world. Skype and Google Hangouts make it possible for students in different states or even on different continents to learn together. Apps like Remind, ClassDojo, and Bloomz enable teachers to stay connected with families, giving parents a real-time glimpse into the classroom, and adaptive software helps make the task of differentiating instruction a bit easier.

This is an exciting time for education to be sure. But as great as all that is, and make no mistake, the tools mentioned above are fantastic, we cannot forget the most important thing in education.

You.

There is nothing more important than you. Nothing can take the place of a great teacher. Nothing. One of my former principals used to say the best teachers could teach under a tree if they had to. Strip away all the things listed above and you're left with the students and their teacher, the most powerful resource there is.

When I was in the classroom, I was sometimes asked two questions by parents whose students were going to be absent for more than a few days:

> Is he going to miss anything important?
> Can you send home what he is going to miss?

While I know the parents were well-meaning and didn't want their students to fall behind, the answer to the first question is, "*Yes.*" Is he going to miss anything important? Uh, yeah. He's going to miss me. He's going to miss time with his teacher. At the elementary level, that's six hours a day. He's going to miss the strategically designed instruction, feedback, and encouragement that come along with me. He's going to miss a lot.

Can I send home what he's going to miss? No, because not only is he going to miss instruction, he's going to miss opportunities to build interpersonal communication skills by interacting with his classmates. That can't be sent home. Sure, I may be able to send home some work, but if it were as easy as sending home a bunch of worksheets, there would be no need for teachers. School is so much more than textbooks and worksheets.

See, a piece of software can never create the feeling a student gets when the teacher or principal speaks his or her name. It can't make a student feel special the way a human voice can.

An iPad or Chromebook can't build a relationship with a student, can't make that student feel loved.

A textbook can't look a student in the eyes and say, "I believe in you. You can do this."

A worksheet can't wipe away the tears after falling and skinning a knee on the playground.

But you can. You can be the difference in a child's life.

We Preach What We Need to Hear

My favorite musical group of all time is U2, and recently I was watching a video in which Bono, the band's lead singer, was explaining the meaning behind their song "Get Out of Your Own Way." He was saying the song was written as letters to their daughters, but then he added, "But like everything, you preach what you need to hear."

Every evening when I come home from work, my wife asks how my day went. On most days my response is positive, but if I'm being honest, there are those when I have difficulty responding in the affirmative and not because it was a particularly rough day with student discipline or contained some other challenge. On the contrary, it's often the days that many would consider to be smooth that are the days I come home feeling a bit down. Why? Because on those days I sometimes feel like I didn't make a difference. If it was an "easy" day, did I really accomplish anything?

In writing this book, I've preached what I sometimes need to hear myself. I have been reminded that there will be days when we feel like we're making a difference and days when we don't. But that doesn't mean a difference isn't being made.

Can you relate? Have you ever asked yourself, *what am I accomplishing with my students?* Ever wondered if you're really making a difference? If you have, I'm here to emphatically tell you that you are!

STORIES OF EDUINFLUENCE

Making a difference in the lives of children is like love — just because you don't feel it doesn't mean it's not there.

If you're married or in a relationship, you know there will be times when you don't experience those lovey-dovey feelings. There will be times when you don't "feel the love," but that doesn't mean the love isn't there. The same is true in education. You don't have to feel the difference to know in your heart you're making it.

You are mighty. Like an educational superhero, you wield incredible power, able to change lives with as little as a single word or simple glance. My message is simple — do not underestimate your impact. Believe in your students. Use their names to create "I'm special" moments. Put relationships above rules. Set an example worth following. Express appreciation. Apologize. Remember the little things. Follow your heart. Make others better by sharing. Go the extra mile. And last, but certainly not least, have fun.

Thank you for reading, and thank you for all you do to invest in the lives of those you serve. They are better because of you. Please don't ever forget that. If necessary, keep this book visible on your bookshelf or nightstand. Pull it out and reread a chapter or two when you doubt your impact. Superman forgetting he possesses the ability to fly, stop bullets and save those in danger would be no good for the world. In the same way, you forgetting the power you possess is no good for the educational world, for the students and adults in your care. May this book serve as the "S" on your chest, or perhaps more appropriately, the "E" for EduInfluencer.

The Powers of EduInfluence

The Power of a Name
There is power in speaking a person's name.

The Power of Relationships
Relationships are more important than rules.

The Power of Example
Our students watch everything we do.
What an opportunity!

The Power of Sharing
Right now, someone is searching for what you have.
You are somebody's Tony Vincent.

The Power of Belief
Belief is the first step toward success or failure,
in our students and in ourselves.

The Power of Apology

We're going to make mistakes with our students.
How we respond afterward is the key to minimizing
the impact of those mistakes.

The Power of Appreciation

Expressing appreciation does for those around us
what helium does for balloons — it lifts them up.

The Power of the Little Things

Sometimes the little things make the biggest impact.

The Power of Fun

We cannot abandon fun in the name of learning.
The two are not mutually exclusive.

The Power of Conviction

Doing the right thing may look wrong
in some people's eyes.

The Power of the Extra Mile

Going the extra mile is worth it,
even if it only benefits a single person.

Acknowledgments

Where would I be without my Professional Learning Network (PLN)? I can honestly say I have learned more from my PLN since joining Twitter in 2009 than I have in 23 years of combined organized professional development. That's not a knock on traditional PD, as I've experienced some of the best, but rather a testament to the power of collaboration through social media. I would not be the educator I am today without the inspiration, encouragement, and resources shared daily by the members of my PLN, many of whom I've never even met in person. Thank you to everyone who pushes me to grow. We are better together!

Sarah Thomas, thank you for believing in my message and for giving me the opportunity to share my stories with the world. You gave me my shot as an author, and for that, I will be forever grateful.

Jennifer Wagner, John Eick, Rushton Hurley, Weston Kieschnick, Cori Orlando, and Ann Kozma, thank you for giving so freely of your time to read and offer feedback on early drafts of the book. I admire and respect each of you immensely, so your advice and words of encouragement were appreciated more than you know.

ACKNOWLEDGMENTS

John Eick, my goal for this book was to encourage and inspire, and I do not know anyone who personifies encouragement and inspiration more than you. Having your words open the book is the highest of honors for me. Thank you, my friend!

And to the staff of Alta Murrieta, thank you for exercising your EduInfluence each and every day for our students. Seeing your dedication and "whatever it takes" attitude in action is a joy to behold. Working alongside you is a privilege I do not take for granted. #AltaRocks

References

Introduction

Future of Storytelling. (2012, October 03). Empathy, Neurochemistry, and the Dramatic Arc: Paul Zak at the Future of StoryTelling 2012. Retrieved from https://www.youtube.com/watch?time_continue=142&v=q1a7tiA1Qzo

Zak, P. J. (2013, December 17). How Stories Change the Brain. Retrieved from https://greatergood.berkeley.edu/article/item/how_stories_change_brain

Chapter 1

Seinfeld (TV Series 1989–1998). (n.d.). Retrieved from http://www.imdb.com/title/tt0098904/

Seinfeld - The Pick. (2017, August 20). Retrieved from http://www.youtube.com/watch?v=iRBH4GmQLDU

Chapter 2

Orlando, C. (2018, March 24). From Happy Face to Heartbreak... [Web log post]. Retrieved from https://leadinginlimbo.weebly.com/leading-in-limbo/from-happy-face-to-heartbreak

REFERENCES

Pierson, R. (2013). Every kid needs a champion. Retrieved from http://www.ted.com/talks/rita_pierson_every_kid_needs_a_champion

Chapter 3

Cast Away (2000). (n.d.). Retrieved from http://www.imdb.com/title/tt0162222/

Chapter 4

Coley, B. (n.d.). Flowchart Notes. Retrieved from http://www.brentcoley.com/flowchart-notes.html

Chapter 5

Dead Poets Society. (1989, June 09). Retrieved from https://www.imdb.com/title/tt0097165/
Stand and Deliver. (1988, March 11). Retrieved from https://www.imdb.com/title/tt0094027/

Chapter 9

The Dark Knight. (2008, July 16). Retrieved from https://www.imdb.com/title/tt0468569/

Chapter 10

Dweck, C. S. (2016). *Mindset: The new psychology of success.* New York: Ballantine Books.

Chapter 11

Coley, B. (n.d.). StudyCast. Retrieved from http://www.mrcoley.com/studycast

Chapter 12

BBC Music. (2017, December 19). U2 - Get Out of Your Own Way (U2 at the BBC). Retrieved from https://www.youtube.com/watch?v=DG20hMiGbSk

About the Author

Brent Coley began his career in education in 1996, teaching grades four and five for 15 years before transitioning into administration. He is currently the proud principal of Alta Murrieta Elementary School in Murrieta, California.

Passionate about educational technology, Brent is always looking for new ways tech can engage students and families while increasing student achievement. His award-winning classroom website, **mrcoley.com**, promoted 24/7 learning with math review videos and iPod flash cards, and his students shared their learning

ABOUT THE AUTHOR

with the world through their daily blog and classroom podcast. In his leadership role, Brent strives to support teachers as they pursue excellence by integrating technology and taking risks in their classrooms.

A firm believer in the power of collaboration, Brent shares what he learns through Twitter (@brentcoley), his website at **BrentColey.com**, and at educational technology conferences. He is also the creator of "Teaching Tales," a podcast that gives educators a platform to share their stories and experiences.

When not working, Brent loves spending time with his wife and two teenage children, reading, and playing golf.

Other EduMatch Books

EduMatch Snapshot in Education (2016)
In this collaborative project, twenty educators located throughout the United States share educational strategies that have worked well for them, both with students and in their professional practice.

The #EduMatch Teacher's Recipe Guide
Editors: Tammy Neil & Sarah Thomas

Hey there, awesome educator! We know how busy you are. Trust us, we get it. Dive in as fourteen international educators share their recipes for success, both literally and metaphorically! In this book, we come together to support one another not only in the classroom, but also in the kitchen.

OTHER EDUMATCH BOOKS

EduMatch Snapshot in Education (2017)

We're back! EduMatch proudly presents Snapshot in Education (2017). In this two-volume collection, 32 educators and one student share their tips for the classroom and professional practice. Topics include culture, standards, PBL, instructional models, perseverance, equity, PLN, and more.

Journey to The "Y" in You by Dene Gainey

This book started as a series of separate writing pieces that were eventually woven together to form a fabric called The Y in You. The question is, "What's the 'why' in you?" Why do you? Why would you? Why should you? Through the pages in this book, you will gain the confidence to be you, and understand the very power in what being you can produce.

STORIES OF EDUINFLUENCE

The Teacher's Journey by Brian Costello

Follow the Teacher's Journey with Brian as he weaves together the stories of seven incredible educators. Each step encourages educators at any level to reflect, grow, and connect. The Teacher's Journey will ignite your mind and heart through its practical ideas and vulnerable storytelling.

The Fire Within
Compiled and edited by Mandy Froehlich

Adversity itself is not what defines us. It is how we react to that adversity and the choices we make that creates who we are and how we will persevere. The Fire Within: Lessons from defeat that have ignited a passion for learning is a compilation of stories from amazing educators who have faced personal adversity head on and have become stronger people for it. They use their new-found strength to support the students and teachers they work with.

OTHER EDUMATCH BOOKS

EduMagic by Sam Fecich

This book challenges the thought that "teaching" begins only after certification and college graduation. Instead, it describes how students in teacher preparation programs have value to offer their future colleagues, even as they are learning to be teachers! This book provides positive examples, helpful tools, and plenty of encouragement for preservice teachers to learn, to dream, and to do.

Makers in Schools
Editors: Susan Brown & Barbara Liedahl

The maker mindset sets the stage for the Fourth Industrial Revolution, empowering educators to guide their students to pursue a path of learning that is meaningful to them. Addressing a shifting culture in today's classrooms, we look to scaling up and infusing this vision in a classroom, in a school, and even in a district.

STORIES OF EDUINFLUENCE

Divergent EDU by Mandy Froehlich

The concept of being innovative can be made to sound so simple. We think of a new idea. We take a risk and implement the new idea. We fail, learn, and move forward. But what if the development of the innovative thinking isn't the only roadblock?

EduMatch Snapshot in Education (2018)

EduMatch® is back for our third annual Snapshot in Education. Dive in as 21 educators share a snapshot of what they learned, what they did, and how they grew in 2018. Topics include purpose, instructional strategies, equity, cultural competence, education technology, and much more!

OTHER EDUMATCH BOOKS

Daddy's Favorites by Elissa Joy
Illustrated by Dionne Victoria

Five-year-old Jill wants to be the center of everyone's world. But, her most favorite person in the world, without fail, is her Daddy. She wants so much to share her ideas, her creations, and most of all, her time. But Daddy has to be Daddy, and most times that means he has to be there when everyone needs him, especially when her brother Danny needs him. Danny is exceptional. He is talented. He is special, and he steals the attention she wants the most. And although Daddy doesn't mean to, sometimes he asks her to share Jilly-Daddy time.

Level Up Leadership by Brian Kulak

From Mario to Lara Croft, gaming has captivated its players for generations and cemented itself as a fundamental part of our culture. Regardless of the genre or platform, one immutable fact connects gaming heroes and the gamers who assume their identities: in order to reach the end of the game, they all need to level up.

STORIES OF EDUINFLUENCE

DigCitKids
Editors: Marialice Curran, Ph.D. & Curran Dee

DigCitKids is digital citizenship for kids by kids. DigCitKids solve real problems in local, global, and digital communities. This book is a compilation of stories, starting with our own mother and son story, and shares examples from both parents and educators on how they embed digital citizenship at home and in the classroom. The stories highlight how learning together and talking with kids — not at kids — is something we all can do, every single day.

www.ingramcontent.com/pod-product-compliance
Lightning Source LLC
Chambersburg PA
CBHW071241070526
44583CB00017B/2285